AN INTRODUCTION TO THE
METAPHYSICAL POETS

D0278877

037840

By the same author

LOSS OF THE MAGYAR
THE SURVIVORS
JUST LIKE THE RESURRECTION
THE ESTUARY
DRIVING WEST
SELECTED POEMS
MRS BEER'S HOUSE
READER, I MARRIED HIM

AN INTRODUCTION
TO THE
METAPHYSICAL POETS

Patricia Beer

Harrow College
Harrow Weald Campus, Learning Centre
Brookshill, Harrow Weald, Middx.
HA3 6RR   0208 909 6248

LEARNING CENTRE

CLASS
NO: 821·4 BEE

ACC
NO: HW 037840

MACMILLAN

© Patricia Beer 1972

All rights reserved. No reproduction, copy or transmission of
this publication may be made without written permission.

No paragraph of this publication may be reproduced, copied or
transmitted save with written permission or in accordance with
the provisions of the Copyright, Designs and Patents Act 1988,
or under the terms of any licence permitting limited copying
issued by the Copyright Licensing Agency, 90 Tottenham Court
Road, London W1P 9HE.

Any person who does any unauthorised act in relation to this
publication may be liable to criminal prosecution and civil
claims for damages.

First published 1972 by
MACMILLAN PRESS LTD
Houndmills, Basingstoke, Hampshire RG21 6XS
and London
Companies and representatives
throughout the world

ISBN 0–333–13667–5 hardcover
ISBN 0–333–29150–6 paperback

A catalogue record for this book is available
from the British Library.

11 10   9   8   7   6   5   4
03 02 01 00 99 98 97 96

Printed in Hong Kong

Contents

Contents

Preface

This book is based on my teaching experience and is intended for students. Although by 'students' I naturally do not mean only those going through the academic mill – I hope anyone approaching the work of the Metaphysical Poets for the first time would find these comments helpful – I do have in mind particular students at a particular stage of their studies, that is, those in their first year of reading for an English Honours degree. The book might also be suitable for pupils in their last year at school, provided they were not just being crammed for A-levels with dictated notes.

From a biographical and bibliographical point of view this introduction does not pretend to offer anything new; to that extent it can be regarded as a compilation. What novelty there is consists, firstly, I should like to think, in the critical remarks; and, secondly, in the fact that every point made is directly founded on some difficulty or query that has arisen in an actual classroom situation.

P. B.

Acknowledgements

The author and publishers wish to thank the following, who have kindly given permission for the use of copyright material:

Faber & Faber Ltd and the University of Chicago Press for the poem 'My Sad Captains' by Thom Gunn from *My Sad Captains*; Faber & Faber Ltd for the poem 'The Gypsy' from *Collected Shorter Poems* by Ezra Pound; New Directions Publishing Corporation for 'The Gypsy' by Ezra Pound, *Personae*, Copyright 1926 by Ezra Pound.

CHAPTER I

The Term 'Metaphysical'

There is not much doubt as to whom we mean when we speak of the Metaphysical Poets. They were men who wrote in a certain manner during the first three-quarters of the seventeenth century, who were led, both chronologically and from the point of view of influence and importance, by John Donne, and whose way of writing came to an end with the poetry of Andrew Marvell and Abraham Cowley. There is considerable agreement about names. No anthology of their work, however select, would exclude the poetry of George Herbert, Henry Vaughan, Richard Crashaw, Thomas Carew and Henry King, and no thoroughly comprehensive collection would omit such minor figures as William Habington, Sidney Godolphin and John Hall. Only occasionally would the selector have to justify some inclusion or exclusion by special pleading.

What right the Metaphysical Poets have to be called metaphysical is another matter and needs comment. The selection of this word as a critical term in the first place was arbitrary. Dryden implied it in *A Discourse Concerning the Original and Progress of Satire*. He says of Donne:

He affects the metaphysics, not only in his satires, but in his amorous verses, where nature only should reign; and perplexes the minds of the fair sex with nice speculations of philosophy, when he should engage their hearts, and entertain them with the softnesses of love.

But he was not suggesting it as a definitive description of a style of writing or of a school of poets. It was Dr Johnson who did that in his *Life of Cowley*:

About the beginning of the seventeenth century, appeared a race of writers, that may be termed the metaphysical poets.

Undoubtedly a word was needed from the beginning to define these poets' clearly recognisable way of expressing themselves. 'Metaphysical' was not the only candidate, however. Professor Helen Gardner, in her introduction to *The Metaphysical Poets*, discusses the term 'strong-lined', which was used by such contemporaries of the poets in question as Robert Burton to indicate not only their kind of writing but also that of certain prose-writers who seemed to show the same characteristics. The word was soon to be as nastily meant as 'metaphysical' was to be by its earliest users but nevertheless it is a reasonably accurate and explanatory term. Sir Herbert Grierson in his introduction to *Metaphysical Lyrics and Poems of the Seventeenth Century*, which presented these poets to the twentieth century with important consequences, puts forward 'fantastic' as a possibility, though only to reject it; this word, too, if properly interpreted, would have been rather suitable.

However unsatisfactory the word 'metaphysical' in this connection may be, it came to stay two centuries ago and will hardly be replaced now. Many critics and most readers, after preliminary reflection and perhaps comment, accept the term without trying to justify it, and use it as one would use any adjective that is no longer particularly informative – like Protestant, Liberal or Georgian – but which serves its purpose in that everyone knows what it refers to.

T. S. Eliot in his essay *The Metaphysical Poets* (in effect a review of Grierson's anthology) after remarking that 'the term has long done duty as a term of abuse, or as the label of a quaint and pleasant taste', is concerned not to discuss its possible accuracy but to define the essential qualities of the poets who are so called. Mrs Joan Bennett, in *Five Metaphysical Poets*, sets herself the same task. She certainly touches on the aptness or otherwise of the name. She admits that Donne, for example, does in fact possess what might be called metaphysical knowledge and draws on it in his poetry but she concludes that 'he is expressing a state of mind by referring to a background of ideas rather than describing the ideas themselves for their own sake', or, as she puts it later (in the chapter specifically on Donne): ' "The metaphysics" occur in his poetry as a vehicle but never as the thing conveyed.' Her real purpose, however, is to analyse metaphysical poetry as we know it and as we accept the term.

Some critics on the other hand have made serious attempts to show that the designation is a justifiable one and no mere tag. (Dr Johnson was not one of them; the aim of *his* argument was to prove, not that these poets were truly metaphysical or otherwise but that they were hardly poets at all.) Sir Herbert Grierson

begins the introduction to his anthology with a round
definition of authentic metaphysical poetry:

> a poetry which, like that of the *Divina Commedia*, the
> *De Natura Rerum*, perhaps Goethe's *Faust*, has been
> inspired by a philosophical conception of the uni-
> verse and the role assigned to the human spirit in the
> great drama of existence.

He admits that 'it is no such great metaphysical poetry
as that of Lucretius and Dante' that he will be dealing
with and, later, speaking of *Paradise Lost*, he states:
'Metaphysical in this large way, Donne and his followers to Cowley are not.' But he would allow them
some claim to metaphysical knowledge, the priests
because of their calling:

> Donne is familiar with the definitions and distinc-
> tions of Mediaeval Scholasticism. . . . The divine poets
> who follow Donne have each the inherited meta-
> physic, if one may so call it, of the Church to which
> he is attached, Catholic or Anglican,

the scholar because of his secular studies:

> Cowley's bright and alert, if not profound mind, is
> attracted by the achievements of science and the
> systematic materialism of Hobbes,

and on the whole he feels the word metaphysical is
apt:

> It lays stress on the right things – the survival, one
> might say the reaccentuation, of the metaphysical
> strain . . .; the more intellectual, less verbal, character
> of their wit compared with the conceits of the

Elizabethans; the finer psychology of which their conceits are often the expression; their learned imagery; the argumentative, subtle evolution of their lyrics; above all the peculiar blend of passion and thought, feeling and ratiocination which is their greatest achievement.

Quite the most interesting discussion of the term 'metaphysical' is that of Professor James Smith in his essay *On Metaphysical Poetry*. He insists that we cannot dispose of the matter simply by saying that Donne and his followers use metaphysical propositions, not seriously as though they were true or at least worth debate, but in order to advance different arguments and beliefs:

> If Donne merely plays ducks and drakes with metaphysics, we may as well abandon our investigation; we shall find a perfectly satisfactory account of him in Johnson.

He claims that Donne's poems deal with subjects of a truly metaphysical nature, for example, 'the stability and self-sufficiency of love, contrasted with the mutability and dependence of human beings' and 'the shortcomings of this life, summarised by decay and death, contrasted with the divine to which it aspires'; and that the treatment of such subjects necessarily leads to the typical metaphysical style:

> For metaphysics, while highly abstract, is by the very reason of its high degree of abstraction intimately concerned with the concrete.

He demolishes most ingeniously the obstacle that has

always prevented readers from thinking that the seventeenth-century metaphysical poets could be metaphysical in the way that Dante and Lucretius were, that is, the fact that they do not sound magisterial and confident, by maintaining that bewilderment and uncertainty in the face of life's problems are in fact part of the essential metaphysical approach. There *ought* to be 'a note of tension or strain'. So by this showing Donne and his school are not less metaphysical than Dante and Lucretius; they are more so.

But however intriguing we may find this argument and to whatever extent we agree with Professor Smith that 'though we may not be saying much when we say that a poem is metaphysical, it is as well to know exactly what the little is we are saying', it is obviously more important to recognise and respond to the unique qualities of the Metaphysical Poets than to argue about the fitness of their name.

Students coming to the work of these poets for the first time are sometimes surprised by the extent to which they themselves thought they were writing differently from the Elizabethans. To a twentieth-century reader the gulf may not seem as great as that between, for example, The Lyrical Ballads and eighteenth-century poetry or between *Prufrock* and Victorian poetry. But Thomas Carew writing in 1631 or 1632 *An Elegie upon the Death of the Deane of Pauls, Dr. John Donne* makes the case seem analogous to these poetic revolutions:

> The Muses garden with Pedantique weedes
> O'rspred, was purg'd by thee; The lazie seeds

THE TERM 'METAPHYSICAL' 7

Of servile imitation throwne away;
And fresh invention planted, Thou didst pay
The debts of our penurious bankrupt age;
Licentious thefts, that make poetique rage
A Mimique fury, when our soules must bee
Possest, or with Anacreons Exstasie,
Or Pindars, not theire owne; The subtle cheat
Of slie Exchanges, and the jugling feat
Of two-edg'd words, or whatsoever wrong
By ours was done the Greeke, or Latine tongue,
Thou hast redeem'd, and open'd Us a Mine
Of rich and pregnant phansie, drawne a line
Of masculine expression.

These are large claims; their magnitude cannot be
accounted for by the fact that Carew himself was of the
school of Donne and might therefore have written in
the possible spirit of a Movement poet of the Fifties
speaking well of another Movement poet whatever he
actually thought. We are so little used to thinking of
the Elizabethan age as being a derelict allotment rank
and overgrown with worthless and boring weeds that
a demonstration of the difference between the two
poetic modes in question might be helpful, even if we
do not come down unhesitatingly on the same side as
Carew. Here are two poems written in the same age
on a very similar theme: Thomas Campion's *When thou
must home to shades of underground* and Donne's *The Apparition*:

When thou must home to shades of underground,
    And there arrived, a new admired guest,
The beauteous spirits do engirt thee round,
    White Iope, blithe Helen and the rest,

To hear the stories of thy finished love
From that smooth tongue, whose music hell can
  move:

Then wilt thou speak of banqueting delight,
  Of masks and revels which sweet youth did make,
Of tourneys and great challenges of knights,
  And all these triumphs for thy beauty's sake.
When thou hast told these honours done to thee,
Then tell, oh tell, how thou didst murder me.

The Apparition

When by thy scorne, O murdresse I am dead,
And that thou thinkst thee free
From all solicitation from mee,
Then shall my ghost come to thy bed,
And thee, fain'd vestall, in worse armes shall see;
Then thy sicke taper will begin to winke,
And he, whose thou art then, being tyr'd before,
Will, if thou stirre, or pinch to wake him, thinke
    Thou call'st for more,
And in false sleepe will from thee shrinke,
And then poore Aspen wretch, neglected thou
Bath'd in a cold quicksilver sweat wilt lye
    A veryer ghost than I;
What I will say, I will not tell thee now,
Lest that preserve thee'; and since my love is spent,
I' had rather thou shouldst painfully repent,
Than by my threatnings rest still innocent.

The Apparition lacks many of the characteristics of the
most typical metaphysical poetry; certainly it has no

claim to be called 'metaphysical' in the full sense of the word that has just been discussed. But to compare it with Campion's poem is to demonstrate some important differences between the two ways of writing.

Both poems announce the same theme in the first line, a theme which was entirely conventional at that time: the death of the loving man because of the savage cruelty of the loved woman. Campion's poem throughout its short length does not depart from this convention: the lover's attitude reveals itself in all its resentment but nothing new emerges in the course of the poem; even the contrived shock of the last line is hardly a surprise. Donne's poem enacts at least three changes of feeling, each one a step away from the Petrarchan convention. His anger at his ill-treatment turns to active and calculated revenge which he thinks out in great detail. The imagined success of his retaliation gives him something so much like pleasure that he takes back the idea with which he must have originally begun – that of threatening her into more complaisant behaviour – as he feels he would enjoy her punishment better than her reformation.

These are interesting glimpses into a man's mind. Psychological insight is not necessary to Campion's poem. It is not intended to be either introspective or subtle. The crack at female heartlessness is boldly and openly delivered, and is not meant to be insidiously penetrating. The speaker, in spite of the strong 'me' ending might be almost anybody. He presents himself simply as a wronged man; in so far as he has any personality at all it is unpleasantly self-righteous; only the women in the poem behave badly.

In *The Apparition* everybody behaves badly, not least the hero, who has a distinct personality. He is dramatically conceived; his own observations on the situation are integrally connected with inferences which we the readers cannot help drawing as part of our response to what he is saying, as we might if we were watching a play. The psychology of lust and resentment is beautifully and faithfully analysed, with its complications and deceptions. The speaker is attractively shameless; he does not attempt to deny the joys of exacting vengeance. Like Heathcliff, when counselled to leave retribution to God, he might have replied, 'God won't have the satisfaction that I shall'. He makes pure spite seem quite a respectable point of view. He is not afraid either to acknowledge the nursery reaction of 'When I'm dead you'll be sorry'; in fact he goes further: in case she is not automatically sorry (he assumes she will not be) he will make her so.

A great part of the poem's strength lies in the discrepancies, psychologically so convincing, which it presents. The whole poem is based on such a discrepancy: that so strong-minded a man would let himself die for love in the first place. There are other realistic contradictions. The last four lines show a mature man indulging in infantile fantasies with such self-awareness that his maturity is not harmed. He sounds perfectly aware, too, of his vanity in supposing that whatever arms she is in they will be 'worse armes' than his. His sexual confidence – though the blow it receives will kill him – is strong enough, or he is hopeful enough, to suggest that the other man will be unable to satisfy her; one attempt by a genuinely frightened woman to wake him up would not result in all that theatrical snoring unless something had previously gone wrong. It is part of the situation, and he maliciously savours the way in which neglect will undermine *her* sexual confidence.

Technically, there are striking differences between the two poems. The static nature of the material in the first is expressed with the smoothness, the regularity and the balance which it needs and which cannot be accounted for completely by the fact that the verses were written to be set to music. *The Apparition*, though metrically far more regular than most of Donne's poems, has none of this rhythmical smoothness. Except for a few trochaic feet the lines are straightforwardly iambic, yet the variety in their length and in their pauses, and above all the speaking voice which transforms them, make the pattern much less obtrusive than Campion's in spite of such noticeable features as the triple rhyme at the end. This question of the speaking voice is a key to much of the technique; anyone in doubt could read aloud the wonderfully sinister line 'What I will say, I will not tell thee now'.

The work of the Metaphysical Poets spans nearly ninety years. Donne was born in 1572 and started writing about twenty years later; Marvell died in 1678. The early work of Donne coincided with some of the most typical Elizabethan poetry; Marvell and Cowley were still writing after the Restoration, when Dryden's career was well under way and Milton's had been ended by death. And these were years of great social and political change. It may seem strained, therefore, to find as many common factors in the work of the Metaphysical Poets as are commonly found, or to see them as a group or a movement at all. But the fact is that they do share certain unmistakable characteristics which can be defined and demonstrated by the critic, and, more importantly, recognised and responded to by the reader. The next chapter attempts to describe some of the most significant.

SUGGESTED READING

Anthologies

Jack Dalglish
> *Eight Metaphysical Poets*, Heinemann, 1961

Helen Gardner
> *The Metaphysical Poets*, Penguin, 1957

Herbert J. C. Grierson
> *Metaphysical Lyrics and Poems of the Seventeenth Century*, Milford, 1921

Criticism

Joan Bennett
> *Five Metaphysical Poets*, Cambridge, 1964

T. S. Eliot
> 'The Metaphysical Poets' in *Selected Essays*, Faber, 1932

Edward Lucie-Smith
> Introduction to *The Penguin Book of Elizabethan Verse*, 1965

James Smith
> 'On Metaphysical Poetry' in *Determinations*, ed. F. R. Leavis, Chatto & Windus, 1934

CHAPTER II

The Chief Characteristics of Metaphysical Poetry

What first strikes most readers of Metaphysical poetry is the fact that so much of it, even after three hundred years and in spite of all the changes in language that such a stretch of time must bring, sounds like people actually talking, that is, the best of it does; the comment applies far less to the minor writers. The speaking voice had of course been represented in non-dramatic Elizabethan poetry:

> With how sad steps, O Moon, thou climb'st the skies!
> How silently, and with how wan a face!
> What! may it be that even in heavenly place
> That busy archer his sharp arrows tries?
> Sure, if that long-with-love-acquainted eyes
> Can judge of love, thou feel'st a lover's case;
> I read it in thy looks; thy languished grace
> To me, that feel the like, thy state descries.
> Then even of fellowship, O Moon, tell me,
> Is constant love deemed there but want of wit?
> Are beauties there as proud as here they be?
> Do they above love to be loved, and yet
> Those lovers scorn whom that love doth possess?
> Do they call virtue there ungratefulness?

The poets were constantly addressing their loved ones or states and objects connected with them such as sleep or the moon, but the effect was, and was intended to be, disciplined and orderly, as in the above sonnet by Sir Philip Sidney. They aimed at a rhetorical not a natural effect. One poem, or rather part of it, the octave, that springs to mind as approaching everyday speech is Michael Drayton's:

> Since there's no help, come let us kiss and part.
> Nay, I have done; you get no more of me,
> And I am glad, yea, glad with all my heart,
> That thus so cleanly I myself can free;
> Shake hands for ever, cancel all our vows,
> And when we meet at any time again,
> Be it not seen in either of our brows
> That we one jot of former love retain;

but though the words sound artless enough the rhythm holds them tightly. It was by rhythm as much as by diction that the Metaphysical Poets achieved the new startling manner, as in, for example, Donne's line:

> For Godsake hold your tongue, and let me love.

There was a great variety of tone, ranging from Donne's impatience to George Herbert's grateful surprise, in *The Flower*:

> Who would have thought my shrivel'd heart
> Could have recovered greennesse?

and Henry Vaughan's informal explanations, in *Man*:

> He knows he hath a home, but scarce knows where,
>   He sayes it is so far
> That he hath quite forgot how to go there.

In these examples the poets speak in their own persons, but in other cases they aim at creating, dramatically, different characters altogether with voices of their own, and here too they are remarkably successful; for example, Andrew Marvell's simple, grieving girl in *The Nymph complaining for the death of her Faun* (where the characterisation is not seriously weakened by the fact that she goes on to mention Deodands and the brotherless Heliades):

> I'me sure I never wisht them ill;
> Nor do I for all this; nor will;

and Richard Crashaw's shepherds, Thyrsis and Tityrus, in *An Hymne of the Nativity*, with their mixture of straightforwardness and sophistication:

> The Babe whose Birth embraves this *morne*,
> Made his own Bed e're he was borne.

> Forbeare (said I) be not too bold
> Your fleece is white, but 'tis too cold;

and the Earl of Rochester's warm-hearted, strong-minded Young Lady in *A Song of a Young Lady. To her Ancient Lover*:

> Ancient Person, for whom I,
> All the flattering Youth defy;
> Long be it e're thou grow Old,
> Aking, shaking, Crazy Cold.
> But still continue as thou art,
> *Ancient Person of my Heart.*

Most of the flexibility and expressiveness of Metaphysical poetry springs – as I have already suggested – from a new freedom of rhythm, the result of poetic

aims very different from those of the Elizabethans.
Donne himself in *The Triple Foole* mentions, as part of
another argument, the limiting effect which verse is
bound to have on the presentation of feelings:

> Griefe brought to numbers cannot be so fierce,
> For, he tames it, that fetters it in verse,

but in his own poetry he sees to it that the limitation
is minimal. In his work, as in that of all the major
Metaphysicals, the metre and verse form are not used
to keep the emotion under control but to enact it:

> O more than Moone,
> Draw not up seas to drowne me in thy spheare,
> Weepe me not dead, in thine armes, but forbeare
> To teach the sea, what it may doe too soone.

The irregularity which this method led to is what these
poets were most severely censured for, by critics
brought up to or preferring the fluency and smoothness of Elizabethan technique.

The Metaphysical Poets really argued in their poetry,
unlike the Elizabethans who, in theirs, tended to stage
debates. A good example of a debating poem is Samuel
Daniel's *Ulysses and the Siren*, in which the two speakers
put forward alternately the pleasures of war and vir-
tuous action and those of peace and selfish rest. Each
point of view is predictable and conventional, and
though to modern ears the siren's pacifist views are
likely to sound more congenial:

> The world we see by warlike wights
> Receives more hurt than good,

contemporary readers were obviously expected to be
on the side of Ulysses, with his notions of honour and
manly exertion:

> Fair nymph, if fame and honour were
> To be attained with ease,
> Then would I come and rest me there,
> And leave such toils as these.
> But here it dwells, and here must I
> With danger seek it forth:
> To spend the time luxuriously
> Becomes not men of worth.

In any case Ulysses is bound to win, and the Siren
accepts her defeat philosophically:

> Well, well, Ulysses, then I see
> I shall not have thee here.

In fact, there is no strain or tension from beginning
to end; that is the charm of the poem.

It is helpful to compare with this poem Andrew
Marvell's *A Dialogue between the Resolved Soul and Created
Pleasure*. The theme is much the same and the form very
similar, except for the addition of a chorus, but the
overall effect of the poem is strikingly different. The
actual arguments propounded are necessarily the traditional ones:

PLEASURE

> Welcome the Creations Guest,
> Lord of Earth, and Heavens Heir.
> Lay aside that Warlike Crest,
> And of Nature's banquet share:

Where the Souls of fruits and flow'rs
Stand prepar'd to heighten yours.

SOUL

I sup above, and cannot stay
To bait so long upon the way

and the outcome is just what might have been expected, but the tone and movement of the poem are
those of real argument, genuine conflict. At one
moment we feel it is almost touch and go as to whether
or not right triumphs:

PLEASURE

Heark how Musick then prepares
For thy Stay these charming Aires;
Which the posting Winds recall,
And suspend the Rivers Fall.

SOUL

Had I but any time to lose,
On this I would it all dispose.
Cease Tempter. None can change a mind
Whom this sweet Chordage cannot bind.

The arguments of metaphysical poetry are not often
presented convincingly by means of two speakers –
there is the delightful exception of Aurelian Townshend's *Dialogue betwixt Time and a Pilgrime* – but frequently
the discussion is so realistic that we seem to hear the
voice and remarks of someone other than the poet,

even if the person is simply a woman capitulating after several verses of vigorous persuasion. An example is Donne's *The Flea*. The presence of the girl is vividly felt throughout and she performs two distinct actions, as it were between the verses: after verse 1 she moves as if to kill the flea; after verse 2 she does so. It is presumed she is not silent either, and in verse 3 her words are actually given in reported speech; ironically, because the very argument by which, as she triumphantly thinks, she has really scored a point against this eloquent suitor is precisely the one he uses finally to subdue her:

Cruell and sodaine, hast thou since
Purpled thy naile, in blood of innocence?
Wherein could this flea guilty bee,
Except in that drop which it suckt from thee?
Yet thou triumph'st, and saist that thou
Find'st not thy selfe, nor mee the weaker now;
  'Tis true, then learne how false, feares bee;
  Just so much honour, when thou yeeld'st to mee,
  Will wast, as this flea's death tooke life from thee.

One of the most characteristic tones of metaphysical poetry is this note of persuasion. John Hall's *The Call* is a much less powerful poem than Marvell's *Coy Mistress* but it is a good routine example of closely-urged invitation, and the scene, the occasion and the people are all dramatically present in the true metaphysical manner:

Romira, stay,
And run not thus like a young Roe away,

No enemie
Pursues thee (foolish girle) tis onely I,
    I'le keep off harms,
If thou'l be pleas'd to garrison mine arms;
    What dost thou fear
I'le turn a Traitour? may these Roses here
    To palenesse shred,
And Lillies stand disguised in new Red,
    If that I lay
A snare, wherein thou wouldst not gladly stay;
    See see the Sunne
Does slowly to his azure Lodging run,
    Come sit but here
And presently hee'l quit our Hemisphere.

The same note of pleading and desire to convince,
though in different circumstances, is heard in William
Cartwright's *To Chloe who wish'd herself young enough for me*
which ends, after urging their complete identification
with each other in love:

And now since you and I are such,
    Tell me what's yours, and what is mine?
Our Eyes, our Ears, our Taste, Smell, Touch,
    Do (like our Souls) in one Combine;
So by this, I as well may be
Too old for you, as you for me.

This verse also illustrates a typical feature of metaphysical poetry: the use of deliberately false logic. If
Chloe was reassured by her lover's argument, it would
have been because of his wish to reassure her, not
because of his method of doing so. There could be no

real confounding of the issue in question: whatever he
said about the fusion of their two selves, the fact re-
mained that she *was* much older than him, in the sense
in which the expression is commonly used, and that
was the sense she apparently cared about. The 'tough
reasonableness' (Eliot's all too famous phrase) of
metaphysical poetry was often the rhetorical reasonableness of quite bogus logic.

It is usually a question of false analogy. Some of the
analogies are literally true; in Edmund Waller's *Go,
lovely rose*, for example: the organic and inevitable loss
of beauty in a rose is a genuine parallel to a woman's
loss of beauty over the years. Others are of a different
kind, as in the last verse of *When, Dearest, I but think on
thee*, attributed to Owen Felltham:

> The waving Sea can with such flood
> Bathe some high Palace that hath stood
>   Far from the Main up in the River:
> Oh think not then but love can do
> As much, for that's an Ocean too,
>   That flows not every day, but ever.

We find this device in Donne's sonnet *Death, be not
proud*: even if dead people and sleeping people did look
alike – which in fact they do not – that would be no
reason for fearing death no more than sleep. We find
it too in his *Sweetest love I do not goe*: the fact that the sun
has further to go than the poet and yet will be back
next day is not much consolation to the wife of a
human traveller, though, as in the case of Cartwright's
poem, the wish to console her may well be.

Harrow College
Harrow Weald Campus, Learning Centre
Brookshill, Harrow Weald, Middx.
0208 909 6248
HA3 6RR

Most of the methods by which the Metaphysical Poets put forward their arguments and their points of view are those used by poets and rhetoricians ever since both arts began and therefore need no description here. There is one, however, which should be singled out because they employed it so distinctively that it is nearly always pointed to first of all as being characteristic of their work, that is, the comparison. All poets use the technique of comparing one thing with another, by means of metaphor and simile, as a way of drawing attention to the essential nature of at least one of the things, but the Metaphysical Poets did it particularly well, with unusual intelligence, wit and emotion. They also looked farther afield than the Elizabethans had done and boldly drew on the whole range of their experience to make comparisons that were so original as to be startling, and at their best so functional as to be far more than decorative.

The best-known comparison of all must surely be Donne's likening of the souls of himself and his wife to a pair of compasses, which is not only arresting but beautifully and accurately worked out. Another famous one is Henry King's simile of the pulse and the drum, which again is brilliantly developed. But they have lost their freshness by too much quotation. Examples from minor writers may illustrate the point better: from John Hall's *On an Hourglasse*:

Poore man, what art! A Tennis ball of Errour;

from Sir John Suckling's *Sonnet*:

What in our watches, that in us is found,
So to the height and nick

> We up be wound
> No matter by what hand or trick;

and from John Cleveland's *To the State of Love*:

> Yet, that's but a preludious bliss;
> Two souls pickearing in a kiss.

(To pickear was to skirmish just ahead of the main body of an army.)

The danger inherent in the use of the striking comparison is obvious from these examples. It is easy to see how the ingenuity could become comic and the originality far-fetched. It is easy, too, to feel the possible justice of Dr Johnson's remark that in the work of these poets 'the most heterogeneous ideas are yoked by violence together'. Professor Gardner has excellently defined the conceit as 'a comparison whose ingenuity is more striking than its justice', and there is no doubt that many of the comparisons of this period must be called conceits, for example this passage from Carew's *Elegy on Maria Wentworth*:

> Else the soule grew so fast within,
> It broke the outward shell of sinne,
> And so was hatch'd a Cherubin.

The difference between a comparison which succeeds poetically and one which does not can best be seen when the comparison is an extended one. If there is not enough poetic intensity to sustain the idea we get such effects as this, from John Cleveland's *The Antiplatonick*:

> The souldier, that man of iron,
> Whom ribs of *Horror* all inviron;

That's strung with Wire, instead of Veins,
In whose embraces you're in chains,
Let a Magnetick girl appear,
Straight he turns *Cupids* Cuirasseer,
Love storms his lips, and takes the Fortresse in,
For all the Bristled Turn-pikes of his chin.

Since Loves Artillery then checks
The brest-works of the firmest sex,
Come let us in affections riot.

If the intensity does not fail we get for example the
beautiful long metaphor, also military, of the flowers
in Marvell's *Upon Appleton House*:

When in the *East* the Morning Ray
Hangs out the Colours of the Day,
The Bee through these known Allies hums,
Beating the *Dian* with its *Drumms*.
Then Flow'rs their drowsie Eylids raise,
Their silken Ensigns each displayes,
And dries its Pan yet dank with Dew,
And fills its Flask with Odours new. . . .

But when the vigilant *Patroul*
Of Stars walks round about the *Pole*,
Their Leaves, that to the stalks are curl'd,
Seem to their Staves the *Ensigns* furl'd.
Then in some Flow'rs beloved Hut
Each Bee as Sentinel is shut;
And sleeps so too: but, if once stir'd,
She runs you through, nor askes *the Word*.

The characteristic wit of Metaphysical comparisons

is easier to recognise than to define. T. S. Eliot's definition – 'a tough reasonableness beneath the slight lyric grace' – is more suggestive than explanatory but it carries the significant implication that the Metaphysical Poets had brains and used them. Their thought was seldom arid. ('A thought to Donne was an experience; it modified his sensibility.') It was precise and exciting, and was as different as could be from vague emotion. Above all it was enjoyable, 'almost fun' Eliot would call it in some cases.

A witty poet can think of more than one thing at a time. A simple demonstration of this is the Metaphysical pun, which resembles the pun of Elizabethan drama and is completely removed from the groan-provoking sort perpetrated by, for example, schoolboys and the Prince Consort. (Professor Empson has given the pun its due as his third type of ambiguity.) It connects things in a meaningful way and with serious intent. The pun on the proper name is significant, especially when it occurs in solemn circumstances, as in Donne's *A Hymne to God the Father* written when he believed himself to be dying:

> When thou hast done, thou hast not done,
> For, I have more.

Even when the theme is light and pleasant the connection between the two elements in the name-pun is no mere prettiness: Aurelian Townshend, comparing a beautiful woman, Lady May, with the spring, ends the poem:

> So smiles the spring, and soe smyles lovely May.

Marvell is a notable user of the pun: in *Upon Appleton House*:

> And now the careless Victors play,
> Dancing the Triumphs of the Hay;

in *An Horatian Ode*:

> The *Pict* no shelter now shall find
> Within his party-colour'd Mind.

So is George Herbert: in *The Pulley*:

> Yet let him keep the rest
> But keep them with repining restlessnesse;

in *Aaron*:

> My onely musick, striking me ev'n dead.

In all these examples the intention and the effect are the opposite of frivolous, though sometimes they may be light-hearted. And this applies to Metaphysical wit as a whole. Eliot after telling us what wit is not ('it is not erudition ... it is not cynicism') says some telling things about it in a more positive mode:

> It belongs to an educated mind, rich in generations of experience . . . it implies a constant inspection and criticism of experience. It involves, probably, a recognition, implicit in the expression of every experience, of other kinds of experience which are possible.

The following lines, taken from Henry King's *The Exequy*, illustrate Metaphysical wit and imagery at their very best:

> Nor wonder if my time go thus
> Backward and most preposterous;

Thou hast benighted me, thy set
This Eve of blackness did beget,
Who wast my day, (though overcast
Before thou had'st thy Noon-tide past)
And I remember must in tears,
Thou scarce had'st seen so many years
As Day tells houres. By thy cleer Sun
My life and fortune first did run;
But thou wilt never more appear
Folded within my Hemisphear,
Since both thy light and motion
Like a fled Star is fall'n and gon,
And twixt me and my soules dear wish
The earth now interposed is,
Which such a strange eclipse doth make
As ne're was read in Almanake. . . .

Sleep on my *Love* in thy cold bed
Never to be disquieted!
My last good night! Thou wilt not wake
Till I thy fate shall overtake:
Till age, or grief, or sickness must
Marry my body to that dust
It so much loves; and fill the room
My heart keeps empty in thy Tomb.
Stay for me there; I will not faile
To meet thee in that hollow Vale.
And think not much of my delay;
I am already on the way,
And follow thee with all the speed
Desire can make, or sorrows breed.
Each minute is a short degree,

And ev'ry houre a step towards thee.
At night when I betake to rest,
Next morn I rise neerer my West
Of life, almost by eight houres saile,
Than when sleep breath'd his drowsie gale.

The Metaphysical style and method could express religious themes as vigorously and as vividly as it could secular subjects, and the development of religious poetry in the first half of the seventeenth century is one of the most distinguished contributions of the Metaphysical Poets to English verse. T. S. Eliot rates this contribution very highly indeed. 'There are those', he says in his essay on Lancelot Andrewes, his tone suggesting that he is one of them, 'for whom . . . the English devotional verse of the seventeenth century . . . [is] finer than that of any other country or religious communion at the time.'

It was an age in which religion was almost certainly the most important preoccupation of both public and private life. Theology was the chief study at the universities. Ecclesiastical intrigue, with its rivalries, alliances and groups, was widespread and notorious. Sermons drew great crowds. Varieties of belief and resulting differences of procedure were followed with interest and discussed with animation, long before the religous confrontation that was so important a part of the Civil War. In their homes men and women who could read studied the Bible and read books of devotion. And in their hearts people worried about their salvation and their standing with God.

All this had been true of the Elizabethan age, but little religious poetry had resulted from it. Now the poets who wrote so well of earthly love, with no change of tone or manner wrote of divine love, in some cases simultaneously, in other cases at different periods of their lives. Most of them had intimate knowledge of religion. A great many were sons of clergymen; a great many were clergymen themselves, of ranks ranging from Bishop to country curate, a long roll-call: John Donne, Henry King, George Herbert, Richard Crashaw, Thomas Traherne, William Alabaster, William Cartwright, Thomas Heyrick, John Norris. And even when religion was not the poet's profession it could be his close concern, as it was in the case of Henry Vaughan, Thomas Carew and Andrew Marvell. It would be wrong to suppose, however, that an air of claustrophobic and unwordly piety pervaded the religious verse of these poets. They knew a great deal about the world and brought this knowledge into their poetry.

The religious verse of Donne, Herbert and Vaughan is well known, and in any case will be discussed later; some extracts from other poets may illustrate better the importance of the religious theme at this time. Thomas Carew, referred to variously by his contemporaries as 'a great libertine', 'that excellent wit' and 'a squire of high degree for cost and bravery', was obviously no recluse, but he experienced intense and recurring anguish about the state of his soul and remorse for his 'Scandalus life', and expressed his real, though intermittent, religious fervour in poems as ardent as *To my worthy friend Mr. George Sandys*:

I presse not to the Quire, nor dare I greet
The holy Place with my unhallow'd feet:
My unwasht Muse pollutes not things Divine,
Nor mingles her prophaner notes with thine;
Here, humbly at the Porch, she listning stayes,
And with glad eares sucks in thy Sacred Layes. . . .
Prompted by thy Example then, no more
In moulds of Clay will I my God adore;
But teare those Idols from my heart, and Write
What his blest Sp'rit, not fond Love shall endite.
Then, I no more shall court the Verdant Bay,
But the dry leavelesse Trunk on Golgotha:
And rather strive to gaine from thence one Thorne,
Than all the flourishing Wreathes by Laureats worne.

What Mr George Sandys had done that so impressed
Carew was to translate the Psalms. The Metaphysical
Poets had a great, and engaging, capacity for admiring
other people. Abraham Cowley's devotion to Richard
Crashaw was the impetus of one of his finest poems,
On the Death of Mr. Crashaw. It is a religious poem, though
free of the soul-searching which inspired Carew. The
vocabulary and the imagery are both those of Christianity: poets are 'the *Poets Militant* Below' and the mas-
ter's Muse 'like Mary, did contain / The Boundless
Godhead'. Crashaw had as an adult been converted to
Roman Catholicism. The idea of his faith illuminates
the whole poem and is made to seem so pleasing that
we are not much surprised to find that Cowley, an
Anglican, not only respects it but can even adopt himself some of the most suspect practices of Catholicism
to do Crashaw homage.

Pardon, my *Mother Church*, if I consent
That *Angels* led him when from thee he went,
For even in *Error* sure no *Danger* is
When joyn'd with so much *Piety* as *His*.
Ah, mighty *God*, with shame I speak't, and grief,
Ah that our greatest *Faults* were in *Belief*!
And our weak *Reason* were ev'n weaker yet,
Rather than thus our *Wills* too strong for it.
His *Faith* perhaps in some nice Tenents might
Be wrong; his *Life*, I'm sure, was *in the right*.
And I myself a *Catholick* will be,
So far at least, great *Saint*, to *Pray* to thee.

An extract from the poetry of Crashaw himself fittingly follows Cowley's praises. *A Hymn to the Name and Honor of the Admirable Saint Teresa* is one of Crashaw's most characteristic and most impressive poems; though he tended to repudiate it as having been written while he was 'yet among the protestantes', it is in fact full of the emotional warmth which seems particularly suitable to his Catholic themes. The sensuous quality of his religious feeling is here seen in all its wealth of 'perfuming' and 'melting' and 'sweetly-killing'.

How kindly will thy gentle HEART
Kisse the sweetly-killing DART!
And close in his embraces keep
Those delicious Wounds, that weep
Balsom to heal themselves with. Thus
When these thy DEATHS, so numerous,
Shall all at last dy into one,
And melt thy Soul's sweet mansion;

Like a soft lump of incense, hasted
By too hot a fire, and wasted
Into perfuming clouds, so fast
Shalt thou exhale to Heavn at last
In a resolving Sigh, and then
O what? Ask not the tongues of men.
Angels cannot tell, suffice,
Thy selfe shall feel thine own full joyes
And hold them fast for ever. There
So soon as thou shalt first appear,
The MOON of maiden stars, thy white
MISTRESSE, attended by such bright
Soules as thy shining self, shall come
And in her first rankes make thee room;
Where 'mongst her snowy family
Immortall welcomes wait for thee.

These poems have been chosen not because they are
the best of their kind (though they are good poems)
but because they are so thoroughly representative of
the religious verse of the time, its range and its skill.
As T. S. Eliot has pointed out in *After Strange Gods*:

The capacity for writing poetry is rare; the capacity
for religious emotion of the first intensity is rare; and
it is to be expected that the existence of both capaci-
ties in the same individual should be rarer still,

so that it is unlikely we shall find much first-class
religious poetry in any one literary period. Yet in fact
in the early seventeenth century we do find it, indis-
putably, in the work of three poets: Donne, Herbert
and Vaughan. These poets, together with Marvell,

were, whatever their subject matter, the greatest of the Metaphysicals and the next four chapters will be devoted to them.

SUGGESTED READING

Maurice Ashley
> *England in the Seventeenth Century*, Penguin, 1952

R. G. Cox
> 'A Survey of Literature from Donne to Marvell' in *From Donne to Marvell*, Pelican, 1956

T. S. Eliot
> 'Andrew Marvell' in *Selected Essays*, Faber, 1932

William Empson
> *Seven Types of Ambiguity*, Chatto & Windus, 1930; Penguin, 1961

Christopher Hill
> *The Century of Revolution*, Nelson, 1961

F. R. Leavis
> 'The Line of Wit' in *Revaluation*, Chatto & Windus, 1936; Penguin, 1964

Basil Willey
> *The Seventeenth Century Background*, Chatto & Windus, 1934; Penguin, 1962

CHAPTER III

John Donne

The most beautiful account of John Donne's life is
Izaak Walton's, written within a few years of Donne's
death; the fullest and most accurate is Professor
R. C. Bald's, published in 1970, well over three hundred
years and two major biographies later. Both make
excellent reading and together leave us with as complete a picture of Donne as we are ever likely to get
now.

John Donne was born in 1572. (The date has been
much disputed but this seems to be the outcome of all
the argument.) His father was a tradesman, but with
connections and ancestry that justified his claims to
gentility, and which enabled his son to mix on more
or less equal terms with anyone he chose. His mother,
Elizabeth Heywood, was the daughter of John Heywood the writer, who had married Sir Thomas More's
niece.

Donne was one of at least six children but by the time
he reached his majority only one of them, his sister
Anne, was still alive. His mother married twice after his
father's death in 1567 but he was lucky with his stepfathers; with the first particularly, a distinguished professional man who made excellent arrangements for
the boy's education, to begin with by private tuition

at home and later at Oxford and almost certainly Cambridge as well.

London was Donne's birthplace and his home or centre for most of his life; his outlook was naturally urban and sophisticated. It is probable that after leaving the University he travelled abroad for about a year, but in 1591 he was back in the capital as a student of law first at Thavies Inn and then at Lincoln's Inn, where he met and made friends with influential men, lived an active social life, read widely in subjects other than law, wrote poetry and examined his own religious standpoint.

Both his parents had lived and died in the Catholic faith – so, it is almost certain, had his stepfathers – and in this faith he had been brought up. It was not easy. He saw much persecution, and of members of his own family. His uncle, Jasper Heywood, a Jesuit and head of the Jesuit mission in England, was arrested in 1583, tried, found guilty and sentenced to death, though the sentence was in fact commuted to permanent exile. Even more painful was the story of Donne's brother, Henry, who was put into prison at the age of twenty for harbouring a priest; under cross-examination he betrayed the priest, and himself died in Newgate soon after. Apart from these tragedies there were lesser trials: Donne knew that any chance of a career would be denied him because of his beliefs. At this stage of his life, when it was most natural to do so in any case, he analysed exhaustively the accepted principles of his youth and emerged from his studies in a mood, if not to recant, at least to feel almost free. From this time onwards he seems not to have been considered as a Catholic, though his Catholic past was held against him in later times of trouble.

Up to this point he apparently had no ideas of a settled profession. He had a little money left him by his father and though it was dwindling there was no real financial emergency as yet. In 1596 there arose a good opportunity to postpone any decisions of this nature as preparations were being made for a large-scale expedition against Spain, led by Lord Howard of Effingham and the Earl of Essex. Donne volunteered and was accepted, and for the next two years (he was a member of the 1597 expedition as well) experienced action, adventure and excitement and witnessed historic events. He also made contacts of a kind which had benefited him so far – friends had introduced him to the Earl of Essex – and would help him even further till the moment when they failed him and went on failing him. Thomas Egerton, probably a friend from Lincoln's Inn days and certainly a friend on the second expedition, used his influence, when they returned home, with his father, recently appointed to the important post of Lord Keeper, to secure for Donne a position as one of his secretaries. The poet seems to have done well in this large and active household, liking the work, which was not only concerned with legal matters but with public affairs as well, and extending his circle of friends. His cynicism about court life and procedure did not entirely prevent his enjoying it.

His prospects of a successful career were auspicious. What ruined them, and for ever, was his clandestine marriage in 1601 to Anne More, niece of his employer

and the daughter of a rich influential country gentle-
man who had so far found rich influential husbands
for three of his daughters and had no wish to change
the pattern. The fury with which he met the announce-
ment of Anne's marriage was not only immense but
practical; he persuaded Egerton to dismiss Donne.
Later he became calmer and made the young couple a
meagre allowance, just enough to live very quietly on,
but could not get his son-in-law reinstated with the
Lord Keeper, who had been reluctant to part with him
but would not now appear so changeable as to take
him back.

From what we know of the marriage it seems to have
been a success emotionally but in every other respect
disastrous. In sixteen years they had twelve children,
Anne Donne's health deteriorating with every birth
until it finally gave way and she died a few days after
the birth of the twelfth child. Throughout these years
both husband and wife were dogged by illness, their
own and that of their children, five of whom died
in infancy or early youth.

Well might Donne refer to their house in Mitcham
as a hospital; the account of this period of his life makes
very depressing reading. He never recovered the favour
which he forfeited by his rash marriage. His friends
were loyal and frequently tried to get him state employment – there was a new court and consequently
a great many openings – but in vain. Chance after
chance went by; promotion followed promotion but
he was left out of it. The patronage of Sir Robert
Drury, with whom Donne spent some time abroad,
led to nothing except the tenancy of a house in Drury

Lane (though that was a great gain) and, surprisingly, neither did that of the much more influential Earl of Somerset.

During fourteen of these sixteen years, though Donne himself was convinced he had no vocation as a priest, many others, including the King, were convinced that he had and were systematically urging him to take holy orders. Their certainty was based on the nature of his character and abilities in general, on the quality of the prose controversies he was writing, as well as poetry, at Mitcham, and on the undoubted fact that to enter the ministry would solve his financial problems. Donne stood out against all these persuasions, partly because he thought so highly of the priesthood as to feel, sincerely, that he was not worthy of it and also because he had so set his heart on a secular career that the long series of disappointments made him only the more determined to win in this field. At last, however, he gave way and in 1615 was ordained at St Paul's.

His advisers had been right. He was a great and immediate success. Preferment and wealth came as surely to him now as they had eluded him for so long. From being appointed Chaplain to the King soon after his ordination he became, in only six years, Dean of St Paul's. He was one of the greatest preachers of all time and, to speak in less worldly terms, developed over the years into a man of deep spirituality whose calling could not be questioned and who used his wide influence with integrity. But he virtually ceased to be a poet. He died in 1631 and was buried in his cathedral amid a roar of eulogy.

It is impossible to date the poems with any accuracy, except for those that deal with known events in Donne's personal life such as his last illnesses, or where the occasion they celebrate is a public one such as a royal death or birth, for example *Elegie upon the untimely death of the incomparable Prince Henry* (who died in 1612) and *An Epithalamion, or mariage Song on the Lady Elizabeth and Count Palatine being married on St. Valentines Day.* (This took place in 1614.) Few except the *First and Second Anniversaries* (1612) were published in his lifetime and these few appeared in anthologies (for example, *Breake of Day* was included in Corkine's *Second Book of Ayres* in 1612), with no reliable indication as to the date of their composition. Sometimes an allusion within the poem tells us something: we know, for example, that *The Canonization* was written after the accession of James I.

But otherwise there is little to go on. Not that that is any great disadvantage, except when, in the past, critics have attempted to date the poems from quite imaginary autobiographical evidence, particularly where the poet's sexual life was concerned: there was a phase of assuming that all the love poems expressing fidelity and peace must have been written after his marriage and all the wild, lecherous ones before it. (There is rather more solid evidence for thinking that the most tortured of the Holy Sonnets were written before his ordination, that is, at Mitcham, and not after it.) Donne's poetry is very much of a piece; he consciously believed in connecting every part of his experience with the rest, and this sense of unity pervades not only each poem but the poems as a whole. It might benefit us very little to know the exact date of each. The first collection of his poems was published in 1633, two years after his death.

To speak of Donne's work in general would be to repeat and apply much of the material of Chapter II. It might be better to give a detailed account of three representative poems.

(a)   *The Funerall*

Who ever comes to shroud me, do not harme
    Nor question much
That subtile wreath of haire, which crowns my
       arme;
The mystery, the signe you must not touch,
    For 'tis my outward Soule,
Viceroy to that, which then to heaven being gone,
    Will leave this to controule,
And keepe these limbes, her Provinces, from
      dissolution.

For if the sinewie thread my braine lets fall
    Through every part,
Can tye those parts, and make mee one of all;
These haires which upward grew, and strength
      and art
    Have from a better braine,
Can better do'it; Except she meant that I
    By this should know my pain,
As prisoners then are manacled, when they'are
      condemn'd to die.

What ere shee meant by'it, bury it with me,
    For since I am
Loves martyr, it might breed idolatrie,

If into others handes these Reliques came;
　　As 'twas humility
To afford to it all that a Soule can doe,
　　So, 'tis some bravery,
That since you would save none of mee, I bury
　　some of you.

In breaking away from an existing convention, the
Petrarchan, Donne often seems to be in the grip of
another, which he has established himself. Certainly
this theme of his body after death is for him a compulsive one, cf. *The Relique* and *The Dampe*. Such a preoccupation is of course in the spirit of his time. In *Whispers
of Immortality* T. S. Eliot, having commented on Webster's
being 'much possessed by death', goes on:

> Donne, I suppose, was such another
> Who found no substitute for sense;
> To seize and clutch and penetrate,
> Expert beyond experience,
>
> He knew the anguish of the marrow
> The ague of the skeleton;
> No contact possible to flesh
> Allayed the fever of the bone.

As Eliot hints, Donne's concern with 'the skull beneath
the skin' is more personal than Webster's and more
complicated than the vision where 'breastless creatures
underground / Leaned backward with a lipless grin'.
His fantasy is both strongly felt and dramatically expressed. There his body lies, surrounded by under-
takers with shrouds, doctors conducting the autopsy,
bishops who have been called in to comment, some-

times even the King, and always gossips and sightseers of every kind.

The particular aspect of the fantasy which *The Funerall* presents, the woman's hair twined round the dead man's arm, is an image which occurs also in *The Relique*, in even more striking words: 'a bracelet of bright haire about the bone'. But the feeling and circumstances of *The Funerall* are different. The lover of *The Relique* has been dead and buried a long time; his grave is being opened up to receive another corpse. The lover of *The Funerall* is awaiting burial; the hair does not look so out of place on a still fleshy arm as it does on a skeleton. And these facts are reflected in the tone of both poems: whereas the first lover in outlasting his flesh feels nothing but pure praise of the lady, the second is near enough to life to keep some very imperfect human emotions, such as bitterness:

> Except she meant that I
> By this should know my pain,
> As prisoners then are manacled, when they're condemn'd to die;

and vindictiveness:

> ... since you would save none of mee, I bury some you.

These feelings recall *The Apparition*. (Though the lover of that poem is a ghost he is an exceptionally lively one, quite unsubdued by death.) But they are muted by comparison.

The two principal metaphors of the poem illustrate the metaphysical manner. In verse 1 the metaphor is doubled: the hair is the 'outward soule', that is, the tangible representative of the inward, invisible soul; it is therefore a viceroy who holds the province (Donne's body) together, while the true ruler (Donne's soul) is absent in heaven. The wit is macabre but almost light-hearted: the dead man's body is on the verge of dissolution and will soon, literally, be falling apart; a wrapping of some kind normally keeps together anything which is falling apart, but a single hair, unless it had magical properties, which this has in the poet's feeling though not in reality, would be comically inadequate to do so. In verse 3 appears the martyr/relic image which is common in Donne's work. It is applied here with reasonable ingenuity and point but its true strength, which redeems it from accusations of blasphemy in the context, comes from what it means to Donne, the intensity springing from youthful pain at the constant danger of martyrdom to which his co-religionists, including close relatives, were exposed.

The tone of the poem throughout is typically Metaphysical, starting with the direct, conversational opening which is all the more startling because in context it is far from being a usual conversational gambit. The second verse is tortuous; the argument is clear enough but because it takes so many turns the expression is inevitably complicated. But suddenly emerging from this subtlety comes the lucid command:

What ere shee meant by'it, bury it with me

after which the poem becomes, intentionally, dense and almost confused again before the final ironical but simple statement.

(*b*)   *Holy Sonnet* XIV

Batter my heart, three person'd God; for, you
As yet but knocke, breathe, shine, and seeke to
    mend;
That I may rise, and stand, o'erthrow mee,' and bend
Your force, to breake, blowe, burn and make me
    new.
I, like an usurpt towne, to'another due,
Labour to'admit you, but Oh, to no end,
Reason your viceroy in mee, mee should defend,
But is captiv'd, and proves weake or untrue.
Yet dearely'I love you, 'and would be loved faine,
But am betroth'd unto your enemie:
Divorce mee, 'untie, or breake that knot againe,
Take mee to you, imprison mee, for I
Except you'enthrall mee, never shall be free,
Nor ever chast, except you ravish mee.

In *The Funerall* Donne uses religious imagery to speak
of sex; in this poem he uses sexual imagery to speak of
religion. The connection between the two subjects is so
basic and so traditional that his method would hardly
call for comment if it were not for the extraordinary
intensity with which he pursues it. Both the intensity
and the fusion of one area of experience with another
are in perfect keeping with what we know of his life
and opinions in general.

The violence of the sentiment is faithfully served by
the technique of the poem, which illustrates the way
in which Donne, and many of the other Metaphysical
Poets, do not state their theme so much as enact it.
The battering which the poet asks God for is felt

throughout the poem; and heard too: it is a very noisy poem. For once we have a genuine example of onomatopoeia. When it is not the sound it is the rhythm: the simile of the siege is comparatively quiet, except for a clattering effect from the 't' sounds, but the rhythm accurately represents the chopping and changing of battle. The first four lines act out their meaning with both rhythm and sound. The poem, like so many of Donne's, works through to a peaceful ending and in this case the sudden tranquillity is very much like the aftermath of sexual strife, in sound as well as meaning.

The poem includes two devices which Donne was fond of using. The first is the catalogue or list:

> . . . . for you
> As yet but knocke, breathe, shine, and seek to
>   mend;
> That I may rise, and stand, o'erthrow mee,' and
>   bend
> Your force, to breake, blowe, burn and make me
>   new . . .
> Divorce mee, 'untie, or breake that knot againe,
> Take mee to you, imprison mee . . .

The effect of the technique in this particular poem has already been suggested: it conveys the idea of a series of demolishing blows. In other poems, as one would expect, its contribution to the whole is quite different, for example in *Holy Sonnet* VII:

> All whom warre, dearth, age, agues, tyrannies,
> Despair, law, chance, hath slaine;

or in *Holy Sonnet* x:

> Thou art slave to Fate, Chance, kings, and
>   desperate men,
> And dost with poyson, warre, and sicknesse dwell,
> And poppie, or charmes can make us sleepe as well,
> And better than thy stroake;

where the list of the things that can kill a man are realistically and precisely enumerated, in the first case to make death seem omnipotent and in the second case to make it seem rather petty. In *Loves Usury*:

> Till then, Love, let my body raigne, and let
> Mee travell, sojourne, snatch, plot, have, forget,
> Resume my last yeares relict;

the subject, that of counting and calculation, is played out in front of us.

The second device is seen in line 6. The use of 'Oh' and 'Ah' in poetry is fraught with great danger. If it succeeds, as in Gerard Manley Hopkins's:

> The heart rears wings bold and bolder
> And hurls for him, O half hurls earth for him off
>   under his feet;

and, to a lesser degree:

> Felix Randal the farrier, O he is dead then?

it succeeds indeed. When it fails, as in Stephen Spender's:

> Was so much expenditure justified
> On the death of one so young and so silly
> Lying under the olive trees, O world, O death?

it fails indeed. These exclamations cannot induce emotion simply because they are emotional exclamations. They have to be integrally connected with the rhythm and the intention of the rhythm, as in Hopkins and Donne.

This poem as a whole demonstrates Donne's handling of metre particularly well. He keeps to the iambic norm which is of course a traditional element in the English sonnet but he treats it as a basis or a starting point from which he continually departs for good poetic reasons of his own. In fact only four of the lines are regular, and one of these, the second, depends on violent elision for its regularity:

> But am betroth'd unto your enemie:
> Divorce mee,' untie, or breake that knot againe. . . .
> Except you'enthrall mee, never shall be free,
> Nor ever chast, except you ravish mee.

The other lines display almost every possible variation of the iambic pattern. There is the trochaic foot:

> Batter my heart . . .
> But is captiv'd . . .
> Take mee to you . . .

There is the strategically placed elision:

> o'erthrow mee,' and bend . . .
> Labour to'admit you . . .
> Yet dearely'I love you . . .

And most characteristically of all there is the foot which is neither iambic nor trochaic for both syllables bear an equal stress (in speaking of English poetry we can hardly use the term 'spondee'):

As yet | but knocke, | breathe, shine, | and seeke | to

mend. . . .

Your force | to breake, | blowe, burn | and make | me

new . . .

(c)   *The good-morrow*

> I wonder by my troth, what thou, and I
> Did, till we lov'd? were we not wean'd till then?
> But suck'd on countrey pleasures, childishly?
> Or snorted we in the seaven sleepers den?
> T'was so; But this, all pleasures fancies bee.
> If ever any beauty I did see,
> Which I desir'd, and got, t'was but a dreame of thee.
>
> And now good morrow to our waking soules,
> Which watch not one another out of feare;
> For love, all love of other sights controules,
> And makes one little roome, an every where.
> Let sea-discoverers to new worlds have gone,
> Let Maps to other, worlds on worlds have showne,
> Let us possesse one world, each hath one, and is one.
>
> My face in thine eye, thine in mine appeares,
> And true plain hearts doe in the faces rest,
> Where can we finde two better hemispheares
> Without sharpe North, without declining West?

What ever dyes, was not mixt equally;
If our two loves be one, or, thou and I
Love so alike, that none doe slacken, none can die.

This poem illustrates beautifully the range and variety of Metaphysical imagery. From the homely activities of breast-feeding and heavy sleeping we pass to the more exotic activities of the explorers, the geographers and the philosophers, from the 'unpoetic' language of:

Or snorted we in the seaven sleepers den?

to the conventionally 'poetic':

Let Maps to other, worlds on worlds have showne.

Some of the images are difficult in the true Metaphysical way:

What ever dyes, was not mixt equally;
If our two loves be one, or, thou and I

Love so alike, that none doe slacken, none can die,
on which most editors give a long note. Other images are touchingly simple:

And make one little roome, an every where.

Several of the metaphors recall those used by Donne in other poems. This in itself is not surprising, but the way in which he makes something new of the same image in order to convey a different experience is worth noticing. In *The good-morrow* the sea-discoverers, with all their topical glamour and novelty, are introduced only to be dismissed as lacking in true exploration compared with the relationship he is describing. Nevertheless they continue to be present in the poem and lead to the image of 'sharpe North' and 'declining West'. In *Hymne to God my God in my sicknesse* the metaphor is pursued for four verses, and illustrates not love but dying. Starting with the visual comparison of himself lying flat in bed with a map over which the doctors/geographers bend and pore, demonstrating that this is his

> South-west discoverie
> *Per fretum febris,* by these streights to die,

he goes on to intellectual speculations in which the east and west of a map bring home to him comforting thoughts about the crucifixion and the resurrection; and through all this reasoning beats the reality of death and, as he thought at the time, of his own imminent death.

The image at the beginning of the third verse of *The good-morrow* is a simple presentation of the fact that people gazing into each other's eyes can see themselves reflected. It is made more complicated and more meaningful by the line which leads up to it:

Let us possesse one world, each hath one, and is one,

and by the line which grows out of it:

And true plain hearts doe in the faces rest,

but on the whole it is simple, as befits a relatively straightforward situation where the 'I wonder ...' is rhetorical rather than truly speculative. In *The Exstasie* on the other hand, where the whole question of the relationship of the soul and body in a love affair is being deeply and literally worked out, the metaphor is much more subtle and bears far more weight:

Our hands were firmely cimented
　　With a fast balme, which thence did spring,
Our eye-beames twisted, and did thred
　　Our eyes, upon one double string;
So to'intergraft our hands, as yet
　　Was all the meanes to make us one,
And pictures in our eyes to get
　　Was all our propagation.

The rhythm of *The good-morrow* reflects the comparative straightforwardness of its subject matter. Lines such as:

If ever any beauty I did see,
Which I desir'd, and got, t'was but a dreame of thee,

are among the most limpid that Donne ever wrote, and nowhere in the poem, except in the last two lines, where the thought becomes knotty, do we meet the irregularities which are a necessary part of many of his themes.

The serene and affirmative note of the poem is one of Donne's many tones. It is neither his most nor his least characteristic voice. He has many, and this variety is an essential part of his work. As his religious poems move through all gradations from confidence to despair and back again, so his love poems present every possible mood. There is the cynicism of:

Though shee were true, when you met her,
And last, till you write your letter,
　　　　Yet shee
　　　　Will bee
False, ere I come, to two, or three;

the contempt of:

> Hope not for minde in women; at their best
> Sweetnesse and wit, they'are but *Mummy*, possest;

the tenderness of:

> But thinke that wee
> Are but turn'd aside to sleepe;
> They who one another keepe
> Alive, ne'r parted bee;

the realism of:

> Who ever loves, if he do not propose
> The right true end of love, he's one that goes
> To sea for nothing but to make him sick;

and the lust of:

> Licence my roaving hands, and let them go,
> Before, behind, between, above, below.

Of all Metaphysical poetry Donne's is the richest and most diverse.

SUGGESTED READING

R. C. Bald
  John Donne: A Life, Oxford, 1970
R. G. Cox
  'The Poems of John Donne' in *From Donne to Marvell,* Pelican, 1956

Frank Kermode
   'John Donne' in *Shakespeare, Spenser, Donne*, Routledge, 1971
Izaak Walton
   'The Life of Dr. John Donne' in *Lives*, ed. G. Saintsbury, World's Classics, 1927

CHAPTER IV

George Herbert

George Herbert had a different start in life from Donne, though later their paths were to cross on several important occasions. Donne was not really hampered by his birth and religion, but Herbert was born, in 1593 at or near Montgomery Castle, to circumstances of the greatest privilege and one might have expected him rather than Donne to end his career as Dean of St Paul's. Herbert's parents were not titled people themselves but they were closely connected with those who were, the Earls of Pembroke, and their family altogether was one of the most distinguished of the time. They were convinced Anglicans, many of them devout. Whatever doubts Herbert may later have had about the nature of his own faith and his suitability for the priesthood he seems to have had no doctrinal scruples or difficulties.

His mother, Magdalen Herbert, must have been a remarkable woman. She seems to have been beautiful, intelligent, good and strong-minded to a quite uncommon degree. She was much admired by exceptional men, such as Donne, and in her widowhood (Herbert's father died when his son was three) she was courted by highly eligible bachelors, the most dashing of whom, Sir John Danvers, she married when she was nearly forty. Her influence on her seven sons appears to have been immense and the strength of her personality may account for a shadowy quality in Herbert's life and career, a dimness from which his poetry escaped.

An aura of ill health and saintliness surrounded him from his youth. He was educated at Westminster School, where he received glowing reports, and Trinity College, Cambridge, where from minor university posts he rose to the positions of, firstly, Reader in Rhetoric and, later, Public Orator. It had been long known that his mother wished him to take Holy Orders, so presumably he was entertaining the idea even while he was winning secular preferment, though it was not until 1625 that he decided to enter the Church. It has been plausibly suggested that Donne was influential here; he was staying with the Danvers family at the time and had been through much the same experience as Herbert, who, in the years before his ordination, had been trying to get advancement in Court circles – in vain, surprisingly, for he was in a much stronger position than Donne had been.

George Herbert, then, was ordained deacon at the age of thirty-two. He did not follow this up by seeking ordination as a priest as soon as he might have. Ill health or religious scruples or the death of his mother, in 1627, may have caused or contributed to this delay. He did not take up parish duties either; the living which was first assigned to him, at Leighton in Huntingdon, was a sinecure and he seems never even to have visited it.

In 1629 he married, very much within the family circle; his bride was Jane Danvers, his stepfather's cousin. It was apparently a happy marriage. In the following year he finally became a priest and accepted the rectorship of Bemerton, near Salisbury. That it should be offered him was not surprising as the living was in the patronage of his relative the Earl of Pembroke; that he should have accepted it was rather strange. The brilliance of his worldly prospects and his own sophisticated manners suggested at all periods of his life some other goal than the cure of this small, secluded parish with its half-ruined rectory and crumbling church.

He stayed at Bemerton till his death in 1633. No one knows the degree of his happiness and peace of mind during these three years, but there is much evidence of his devotion to his duties, his goodness and his piety. As a country parson he was admired and loved, and, to all appearances, he was content.

He had written poetry since his undergraduate days; even so early he had felt a need to use his gift in the service of God. During his years at Bemerton he revised his existing poems and wrote a great many more. The resulting collection was called *The Temple* and was published a year after his death by his friend Nicholas Ferrar, of Little Gidding. While at Bemerton he also wrote a prose work, *A Priest to the Temple*, which describes the responsibilities of a country clergyman and the standards he should set himself.

In the mid-twentieth century two difficulties are bound to stand in the way of the average reader's enjoyment of religious poetry: the first is the obvious one that few people nowadays are religious; and the second is that few people, even if they have received a good general education, know much about the basic facts of Anglican or Catholic belief or at least not enough to appreciate the feelings of those who are disturbed or excited by them or of those who use them as a medium of expression. These are very real difficulties to readers approaching the work of such poets as George Herbert and Gerard Manley Hopkins, who write primarily about religion, even if simple hostility to the subject matter does not add yet a third difficulty. And perhaps a poet like Herbert suffers more from these barriers than Hopkins, whose work often projects a passion that is a-religious. Passion is there in Herbert's poetry. He knew, for example, better than most people what it is to spend a sleepless night in a state of the most cruel anxiety:

> ... I am he
> On whom thy tempests fell all night,

but he records the fact as Jane Austen might (as indeed she does in one passage of *Pride and Prejudice*) without screaming about it, and then goes on to his real point. While Hopkins shrieks, Herbert merely sighs and then not for long.

It is true that anyone discussing virtue can, and to a certain extent must, discuss vice, which interests more people. Preachers and poets extolling chastity have a splendid opportunity to talk at length about lust, as Milton did in *Comus*. But Herbert takes little advantage of such opportunities. He often shows *himself* in an unflattering light, but reticently, and he seldom inveighs against the sins of others.

How then is it possible to enjoy the poetry of Herbert

if we happen not to be the fellow-Christians for whom he was writing? There are at least three ways. The first is summed up in the words of D. J. Enright, who called Herbert 'one of the strongest poetic personalities in English', a phrase well worth thinking over. The second follows from it: a man of strong literary personality who writes his autobiography – and that is what much of *The Temple* is – can hardly help being interesting, and any unfamiliarity in the subject matter could well be an attraction rather than an obstacle. And there is sure to be much that is familiar. Professor Empson, whose remarks on Herbert scattered throughout *Seven Types of Ambiguity* are some of the most illuminating that have been made, pointed out that a poem about religious endeavour (he was speaking specifically about 'I gave to Hope a watch of mine', but the comment could be applied generally) 'may be read so as to convey ... a statement of the stages of, a mode of feeling about, *any* prolonged endeavour; so that the reader is made to accept them all as alike in these particulars, and draw for his sympathy on any experience of the kind he may have had'. Thirdly, there is the skill and beauty of Herbert's craftsmanship; a study of three poems should make this clear.

(a)   *Redemption*

   Having been tenant long to a rich Lord,
     Not thriving, I resolved to be bold,
     And make a suit unto him, to afford
   A new small-rented lease, and cancell th'old.
   In heaven at his manor I him sought:
     They told me there, that he was lately gone

About some land, which he had dearly bought
Long since on earth, to take possession.
I straight return'd and knowing his great birth,
  Sought him accordingly in great resorts;
    In cities, theatres, gardens, parks and courts:
At length I heard a ragged noise and mirth
  Of theeves and murderers: there I him espied,
  Who straight, *Your suit is granted*, said, and died.

The theme of Christ dying for sinners was a favourite of Herbert's; the events leading up to Good Friday and the Crucifixion itself inspired some of his strongest poems, e.g. *The Agonie* and *The Sacrifice*. He clearly preferred Easter to Christmas.

In this poem the subject is presented in the form of a parable, closely modelled on those in the Gospels. The characters and their activities recall Christ's stories: the landlord who has gone to claim a piece of land, the tenant with a suit, the whole set-up of buying and selling. The rhythm and tone of the poem, too, echo the Bible stories:

A certain nobleman went into a far country to receive for himself a kingdom and to return.

The kingdom of heaven is like unto a merchant man, seeking goodly pearls, who when he had found one pearl of great price went and sold all that he had and bought it.

So when even was come the lord of the vineyard saith unto his steward, Call the labourers, and give them their hire, beginning from the last unto the first.

As these quotations are taken from the King James Version it is not surprising that Herbert's poem should sound like them. The degree of resemblance is significant, however, in that it indicates the strength and singleness of Herbert's poetic purpose, which corresponded with his professional purpose: the earnest desire to explain, to reveal, to instruct. The well-worn definition of metaphor as the attempt to convey something unknown in terms of something that is known gets new life, and the metaphor itself added strength, from Herbert's compulsion to transmit his meaning at all costs, a compulsion that is not primarily poetic but vocational, the duty of a preacher to show people the truth so that their souls may be saved. He must use any material that may help:

> The Country Parson is full of all knowledg. They say, it is an ill Mason that refuseth any stone; and there is no knowledg, but, in a skilfull hand, serves either positively as it is, or else to illustrate some other knowledg. He condescends even to the knowledg of tillage, and pasturage, and makes great use of them in teaching, because people by what they understand are best led to what they understand not.

The analogy in this poem is a very well-chosen one. The imagery of manors, rich Lords and leases, which might seem strange and quaint to many mid-twentieth-century English readers, would have been familiar, homely even, to those of the early seventeenth, and the allusion to 'great resorts' would have been acceptable to country-dwellers who even today rather exaggerate the goings-on in big cities and expect to find 'theeves and murderers' there in greater abundance than at home.

The sonnet form in English has not been used for narrative purposes anything like as much as it has been for meditation or the description of states of mind, but it is not essentially unsuited to the telling of a story, as shown by Herbert's use of it here. His story is short and neatly-turned, and the sonnet form is especially right for short, well-structured subjects. Herbert is a good story-teller, as is seen in some of his other poems, e.g. *Love*; and in *Redemption*, though its scope is limited, we see the main features of good narrative. The necessary explanations (the first quatrain) are got out of the way deftly but with clarity, the climax is strong and uncluttered, and the use of dialogue is skilful: the indirect speech of the second quatrain is appropriate in itself, as it suggests the distance of the heavenly manor and the fact that that stage of the venture is well in the past, and it also contrasts with the direct speech of the last line.

This last line comes as a surprise, but not the surprise of ordinary life where something happens which is genuinely unexpected. Herbert, by the very nature of his poetry, could never cause that kind of effect: his stories were universally known; in those days, probably even now, no one could imagine that the rich Lord was *not* going to grant the suit or that he was *not* going to die, neither could anyone who knew anything about Herbert's views suppose that in any poem vice was going to triumph or even put up much of a fight. The surprise that Herbert provides, in many of his poems as well as *Redemption*, e.g. *The Collar* and *The*

Pulley, is the more lasting shock that literature can give, a shock that is so independent of not knowing what is going to happen that it can be felt again and again; in *The Woman in White*, for example, the moment when the hero, standing by the heroine's grave, looks up and sees her alive on the other side of it, can be as unexpected at the tenth time of reading as at the first.

The metre of the sonnet is as suitable to Herbert's subject as its form. The Biblical passages quoted above rely very much for their rhythmic effect on an iambic beat and contain at least two natural iambic pentameters:

> beginning from the last unto the first . . .
> the lord of the vineyard saith unto his steward . . .

so that it is not surprising that the poem should sound fluent and near to the speaking voice of someone persuasively telling a story. The mid-line pauses are particularly well managed so that variety goes with continuity.

(*b*)   *Jordan*

Who sayes that fictions onely and false hair
Become a verse? Is there in truth no beautie?
Is all good structure in a winding stair?
May no lines passe, except they do their dutie
    Not to a true, but painted chair?

Is it no verse, except enchanted groves
And sudden arbours shadow course-spunne lines?
Must purling streams refresh a lovers loves?
Must all be vail'd, while he that reades, divines,
    Catching the sense at two removes?

Shepherds are honest people; let them sing:
Riddle who list, for me, and pull for Prime:
I envie no mans nightingale or spring;
Nor let them punish me with losse of ryme,
    Who plainly say, *My God, My King.*

It is typical of Herbert's method that he should, in this poem and in others, e.g. *The Pulley* and *The Collar*, choose a title which is in a sense self-contained and independent of the poem itself. There is absolutely no mention of or reference to Jordan in these verses. But a little thought, and some knowledge of what the river Jordan might stand for, shows it to be a perfectly apt title. The Jordan was the river of baptism in the days of Christ; it purified and introduced people to a new life. It has also been used, both before and after the time of Herbert, as a symbol of death ('One more river and that's the river of Jordan'), which would lead to the better state of immortality. In view of the theme of the poem it is probably not fanciful to think also of other waters, connected with non-Christian poetry, such as the springs of Helicon.

This poem reaffirms a statement Herbert had made years before. In the New Year of 1610 he had sent his mother two sonnets together with a letter in which he deplored 'the vanity of those many love poems that are daily writ and consecrated to Venus' and the fact that 'so few are writ that look towards God and heaven', and summed up his feelings in the protestation:

My meaning (dear mother) is, in these sonnets, to declare my resolution to be, that my poor abilities in poetry, shall be all and ever consecrated to God's glory.

It was not that then or later he was unmoved by worldly temptations. He says so in *The Pearl*:

> I knowe the wayes of Pleasure, the sweet strains,
> The lullings and the relishes of it;
> The propositions of hot bloud and brains;
> What mirth and musick mean; what love and wit
> Have done these twentie hundred yeares, and more
> I know the projects of unbridled store:
> My stuffe is flesh, not brasse; my senses live,
> And grumble oft, that they have more in me
> Then he that curbs them, being but one to five;

and in *Affliction*:

> Whereas my birth and spirit rather took
> The way that takes the town;
> Thou didst betray me to a lingring book,
> And wrap me in a gown.

Jordan reminds us of Milton's statement in *Lycidas* and his resentment that all his dedication, so unlike the frivolity of others, is yielding him nothing in the way of fame and prestige:

> Were it not better done as others use
> To sport with Amaryllis in the shade
> Or with the tangles of Neaera's hair?

Herbert is not resentful but he is occasionally envious of the ease with which profane poets can achieve their effects. He says in *Dulnesse*:

> The wanton lover in a curious strain
>   Can praise his fairest fair;
> And with quaint metaphors her curled hair
>   Curl o're again.

In *Jordan* Herbert is of course speaking not only of subject matter but of style. It is his manifesto that poetry may be simple, straightforward and free of poetic diction and still be successful. It could not have been that he thought no poetry should be complicated – after all he was a great admirer of Donne – but that he believed some subjects demanded simplicity both for artistic reasons and so that the moral might be understood.

It was an essential part of Herbert's nature to practise what he preached and this poem is the best kind of critical statement in that it actually demonstrates the point while formulating it. (The same applies to the second *Jordan* poem which is a companion piece and should be read alongside the first.) The demonstration is twofold: when Herbert is speaking about the other sort of poetry he parodies its vocabulary in such phrases as 'enchanted groves' and 'purling springs', expressions quite foreign to his own way of putting things.

The simplicity he advocates is present in every aspect of *Jordan*. The movement is almost naïve: the first two verses consist of a series of rhetorical questions which are even less like real inquiries than most rhetorical questions; they demand not the ghost of an answer. And in fact they do not get one here; the straightforward, highly affirmative third verse does not treat them as serious or subtle and seems to cut them off rather than deal with them.

The symbols are equally obvious, in the best sort of way: the winding stair, the painted chair, the shepherds, and particularly those of the superb line:

I envie no mans nightingale or spring,

where images which are trite in themselves, even separately and especially together, are deliberately chosen and so managed as to create a strength and freshness which is typical of Herbert.

(c) *Death*

Death, thou wast once an uncouth hideous thing,
    Nothing but bones,
  The sad effect of sadder grones;
Thy mouth was open, but thou couldst not sing.

For we consider'd thee as at some six
    Or ten years hence,
  After the losse of life and sense,
Flesh being turn'd to dust and bones to sticks.

We lookt on this side of thee, shooting short;
    Where we did finde
  The shells of fledge souls left behinde,
Dry dust, which sheds no tears, but may extort.

But since our Saviours death did put some bloud
    Into thy face;
  Thou art grown fair and full of grace,
Much in request, much sought for as a good.

For we do now behold thee gay and glad,
    As at dooms-day;
  When souls shall wear their new aray,
And all thy bones with beautie shall be clad.

Therefore we can go die as sleep, and trust
    Half that we have
  Into an honest faithfull grave;
Making our pillows either down, or dust.

In the chapter on Herbert in *Five Metaphysical Poets* Joan Bennett compares this poem with a section of *In Memoriam* and it is perhaps an even better demonstration of T. S. Eliot's much-quoted theory of 'dissociation of sensibility' than Eliot's own examples. The comparison is fair (the *In Memoriam* passage is a fine one) but Tennyson's verses do suffer from it. It is true that Tennyson was at a disadvantage when discussing immortality as he lived in a time of doubt, and in fact we know from the poem as a whole that his strongest argument was not more satisfactory than: 'If there were no such thing as immortality I could not bear life, therefore there must be immortality.' Herbert really believed. But that is possibly irrelevant, for had Herbert been the poet with doubts and Tennyson the one with certainty Herbert might still have had the advantage, his language is so precise and strong, violent even, compared with Tennyson's beautiful and gentle musings.

The basic structure of the poem is simple and symmetrical: three verses to show what death was like before the Resurrection of Christ, and three verses to show what it has been like since. But the poem as a whole is complicated by the quick and ambiguous way in which Herbert glances from one aspect of his subject to another, his mind, as Professor Empson puts it, 'jumping like a flea'.

Death starts as a person, but not the arrogant killer humbled by the coming of Christ that Donne sees. He – and it is convenient rather than accurate to say 'he' about someone who is as sexless as an angel – is first seen as a dead person with all the realistic and gruesome attributes of a corpse: open mouth, putrefaction, ugliness. These details are strengthened by the grotesque fantasy at the end of verse 1; we know that a corpse, except in legend, cannot sing, but we may not have thought of the likeness of a mouth that has sagged in death to a live singing mouth, and we now see the dead mouth all the more clearly.

In verse 3 death becomes more like a place; on this side of it we find the eggshells, dry and brittle, which the souls like baby birds have left behind. (A lively image; poets often liken souls to birds – Marvell does – but seldom to baby birds.) What is beyond death and where the souls have gone is left alarmingly vague. Here, too, we have the grotesque negation. Again, it hardly surprises us that dry dust sheds no tears, but it helps to be made to imagine the aching frustration and strain of trying to squeeze something indicative of life and emotion out of something that has neither.

As the second half of the poem opens death becomes a person again, this time a live person, healthy, handsome and popular. The transfusing process by which the blood of Christ enters his pale face is not stressed but has suggestions as grotesque as any of the others in the poem. Death then merges into other live, attractive people, the risen souls at the last Resurrection, when both he and they will be well-dressed and radiant.

In conclusion the argument shifts to the traditional comparison between death and sleep, and momentarily the intensity of the poem slackens, but the vitality of the last three lines completely revives it. To call the body 'half that we have' is a fresh way of indicating the soul/body relationship, hackneyed as this theme was. 'The honest, faithfull grave' where we sleep has the domestic charm of a peaceful marriage bed, even before the final comfortable touch of the down pillows in the last line.

Herbert's mental agility and his refusal to present only one facet of his subject at a time are what make the poem so convincing. It is an excellent example of the 'hopping' technique so characteristic of Metaphysical poetry, and particularly of Herbert.

SUGGESTED READING

Margaret Bottrall
  George Herbert, John Murray, 1954
D. J. Enright
  'George Herbert and the Devotional Poets' in *From Donne to Marvell*, Pelican, 1956
L. C. Knights
  'George Herbert' in *Explorations*, Chatto, 1951
J. H. Summers
  George Herbert, Chatto, 1954
Izaak Walton
  'The Life of Mr. George Herbert' in *Lives*, ed. G. Saintsbury, World's Classics, 1927

CHAPTER V

Henry Vaughan

Henry Vaughan was born at Newton near the River Usk in Breconshire in 1621 and in this remarkably beautiful part of the country he passed his life, except for two years at Oxford, from 1638 to 1640, and the two years after that when he was studying law in London. He was proud of his descent and liked to call himself 'Silurist' after the Silures, the tribe who inhabited those parts in Roman times. His father was a man of good family with a small estate which Henry Vaughan, the elder of twin brothers, later inherited.

He married, suitably, in 1646 and settled on the family estate. At this stage in his life his attitudes seemed fixed, and of a kind unlikely to disrupt what promised to be a peaceful, prosperous existence. He was a convinced Royalist; he may possibly have fought for the Cause at some point but his service could not have lasted long and it got him into no trouble. He was a practising Anglican, but his religion was not of an uncomfortable or soul-searching variety. He was deeply fond of the country he lived in. And to occupy his mind and talents he wrote poetry.

His first book of poems was published when he was twenty-five. His themes were secular and for a model he turned chiefly to Donne, and he did not merely

imitate, he stole. Some of his thefts are startlingly
unsubtle and show how much it must have been the
custom of the time to lift whole verses, only slightly
recast, from the poetry of others. Here is an extract
from one of the Amoret poems:

> Just so base, Sublunarie Lovers hearts
>   Fed on loose prophane desires,
>   May for an Eye,
>   Or face comply:
> But those removed, they will as soone depart,
>   And shew their Art
>   And painted fires.
>
> Whilst I by pow'rfull Love, so much refin'd
>   That my absent soule the same is
>   Carelesse to misse,
>   A glaunce, or kisse,
> Can with those Elements of lust and sence,
>   Freely dispence,
>   And court the mind.

Such flagrant borrowing, however much in keeping
with the contemporary spirit, did point to lack of
strong personal impetus where poetry was concerned,
and in fact the poems included in this first volume were
the work of an intelligent, educated man who could
write verses with the best, rather than anything more
compulsive.

Between 1646 and the publication of the first edition
of *Silex Scintillans* in 1650 a great change came. Vaughan
experienced what could loosely be called religious
conversion. What caused it is not known. Several cir-

cumstances can be pointed to as probably contribu-
tory: the defeat of the Royalist cause, the subjection,
particularly in South Wales, of the Anglican Church,
a serious illness of the poet's; and, most poignant of all,
his poems seem to indicate, the death of his brother
William.

Vaughan's new awareness of God provided him with
the important central experience which up to now he
had lacked, and from now on his religious faith co-
ordinated and made sense of everything he observed
and felt. Many people, of course, have undergone
conversion, sometimes dramatically like St Paul,
without becoming great religious poets. Vaughan
already had the potential; he now had the subject
matter and the inspiration.

He himself, in the preface to the second, 1655, edition
of *Silex Scintillans*, attributes his new attitudes both as a
man and a poet to the influence of 'that blessed man
Mr. George Herbert, whose holy *life* and *verse* gained many
pious *Converts* (of whom I am the least)'. This tribute is
honest and generous but not entirely necessary, as the
influence of Herbert is plainly to be seen in Vaughan's
poetry. As Vaughan's biographer, Dr Hutchinson,
comments, 'There is no example in English literature
of one poet borrowing so extensively from another'.
But when all Vaughan's borrowings have been listed
and discussed, we are left with a poetic personality that
is completely individual and independent, and,
strangely, as unlike Herbert's as could well be.

Domestically Vaughan's life was full. He had four
children by his first wife and on her death he married
her sister and begot four more children. When the

children of the first marriage grew up there were
various quarrels and lawsuits about property and in
fact his eldest son took over Newton during his father's
lifetime. But though Vaughan was in this way deprived
of a landowner's activities he pursued an exacting
professional career as a doctor to the end of his life.
Nothing is known of his medical qualifications. We do
know that from the age of about thirty he had studied
and indeed translated treatises on the medical implica-
tions of Hermeticism but his lifelong interest in medi-
cine may not have been consolidated by any formal
training. But even if he was not properly qualified at
all he was a very popular and successful doctor, and his
practice included the most important people in the
district.

He died in 1695 and was buried in the beautiful
churchyard of Llansantffraed.

(a)   *The Showre*

'Twas so, I saw thy birth: That drowsie Lake
From her faint bosome breath'd thee, the disease
Of her sick waters, and Infectious Ease.
    But, now at Even
    Too grosse for heaven,
Thou fall'st in teares, and weep'st for thy mistake.

Ah! it is so with me; oft have I prest
Heaven with a lazie breath, but fruitles this
Peirc'd not; Love only can with quick accesse
    Unlock the way,
    When all else stray
The smoke, and Exhalations of the brest.

Yet, if as thou dost melt, and with thy traine
Of drops make soft the earth, my eyes could weep
O're my hard heart, that's bound up, and asleep,
   Perhaps at last
   (Some such showres past,)
My God would give a Sun-shine after raine.

The subject of this poem, the need of the soul to communicate with God, is one which Donne and Herbert had attempted, too, in their very different ways. Vaughan here shows himself to be different in his approach from both of them. His method is to explore the theme by way of his observation of nature. The description of the mist rising from the lake, hanging over it oppressively all day, and finally at evening falling in rain is convincing and impressive. Already in this first verse there are strong hints of a more serious meaning: suggestions of laziness and unhealthiness in the mist itself and the lake that formed it and a clear statement that it fails to rise farther not because there is no wind but because it is too gross.

The analogy which forms the main part of the poem is introduced explicitly at the beginning of verse 2, 'Ah! it is so with me,' and then expounded straightforwardly. The third verse is a hopeful conclusion to the argument: the falling of the rain suggests the possibility of remorseful tears leading to a softer and more receptive attitude, so that at last in his spiritual life as in the scene he is describing there may be sunshine after rain.

The poem is very neatly planned and constructed. Vaughan is often accused of lacking a sense of form but

The Showre, and a great many other poems of his, can stand comparison with Herbert in this respect.

The connection between rain and penitential tears, between sunshine and spiritual birth is in itself conventional and trite; but the poem as a whole is not. In the first place, Vaughan avoids generalisations in his descriptions of nature. It is not any shower or all showers he is using to make his point. It is one particular one, as he makes clear from the immediacy of his first words, ' 'Twas so, I saw thy birth' (a characteristic metaphysical opening), which have the argumentative tone of one who is prepared to establish the accuracy of what he is saying. In the second place, the poem creates a powerful atmosphere, which appeals to all the senses. Considering there is so little detail it is surprising how vividly we experience the scene, The explanation must lie in Vaughan's identification, at a deep level, of religious concepts with the things of nature. Certainly the rain and sunshine imagery is an essential part of his thinking.

The verse form, with its striking shape, its regular metre and prominent rhyme scheme, has inevitably a rather cramping effect on the rhythm. Vaughan often sets himself this sort of problem and usually solves it: where the rhythm cannot make as great a contribution as it might, other devices – a well-handled rhyme, a sound effect – can make another sort of point. In this poem his management of the syntax provides some rhythmical variety, of a kind which is helpful to the meaning. The first two verses, which set out the situation, have a strong syntactical pause about halfway through, after 'Infectious Ease' in the first verse and

after 'Peirc'd not' in the second. The third verse, however, presenting the conclusion, starts with two sub-
ordinate clauses, 'if as . . .', which carry it on with
considerable sweep and with hardly a pause into the
final telling statement.

(b)   *Come, come, what doe I here?*

> Come, come, what doe I here?
>   Since he is gone
> Each day is grown a dozen year,
>   And each houre, one;
>   Come, come!
>   Cut off the sum,
> By these soil'd teares!
>   (Which only you
>   Know'st to be true,)
> Dayes are my feares.
>
> Ther's not a wind can stir,
>   Or beam passe by,
> But strait I think (though far)
>   Thy hand is nigh;
>   Come, come!
>   Strike these lips dumb
> This restless breath
>   That soiles thy name,
>   Will ne'r be tame
> Untill in death.
>
> Perhaps some think a tombe
>   No house of store,
> But a dark, and seal'd up wombe,
>   Which ne'r breeds more.

> Come, come!
> Such thoughts benum;
> But I would be
> With him I weep
> A bed, and sleep
> To wake in thee.

This poem is one of nine from *Silex Scintillans* which are not printed together but are clearly linked, not only by their subject matter but by the external fact of the paragraph mark which introduces them. The finest of them is the well-known 'They are all gone into the world of light', which speaks of the death of many friends. This poem, and 'Silence and stealth of dayes', which should be read with it, lament more particularly the death of Vaughan's brother William. The almost certain connection between this bereavement and Vaughan's religious conversion adds to the interest of the poems.

'Come, come, what doe I here?' is slight compared with 'They are all gone into the world of light' and even with 'Silence and stealth of dayes', and is circumscribed by its close metrical pattern. But its very spareness reveals many of Vaughan's best skills. The rhythm, for example: one would think that a series of such short lines so weighted with rhyme could hardly permit any rhythmic variation but in fact the last five lines of each verse show considerable freedom and subtlety. The first verse ends solidly with a strong free-standing statement, 'Dayes are my feares'. The last four lines of the second verse almost run down the page in a way which perfectly enacts the flowing away of life. The

ending of the third verse is different again. The strong
pause in the penultimate line and consequent blurring
of the rhyme is comparable with Donne's way of con-
cluding 'Sweetest love I doe not go ...'

> But thinke that wee
> Are but turn'd aside to sleepe;
> They who one another keep
> Alive, ne'er parted be.

In both cases the carrying over of the sense of one line
to the beginning of the next disrupts the metrical
pattern in a way which gives greater prominence to the
meaning, and as in both cases the chief weight of the
sense falls just here this is highly effective.

Vaughan's poem is a simple statement of loss, free
of any speculation about immortality or eternity; such
speculations we can find elsewhere in his work. He
touches on two possible views of the grave, which may
be regarded as either a storehouse, with all the conno-
tations of future prosperity which the metaphor
evokes, or as a womb that has become barren and will
never yield life any more. He dismisses this second
metaphor only because 'such thoughts benum', not
because he has conquered them. He then quite openly
regresses to childhood and wishes that he and his
brother were back in bed together, with a lifelong sleep
protecting him from sorrow.

As Vaughan frequently uses natural imagery to convey religious experience, so he uses it here to speak of
human emotion. 'The touch of a vanished hand' has
been one of the greatest symbols of loss in literature.

Tennyson uses it not only in *Break* but also in *In Memoriam*:

> Dark house, by which once more I stand
> Here in the long unlovely street,
> Doors, where my heart was used to beat
> So quickly waiting for a hand
>
> A hand that can be clasp'd no more . . .

But the circumstances which bring to Tennyson the thought of the lost hand are the realistic circumstances of everyday life, a house with a door that will open to permit the natural handshake of a friend. The hand which Vaughan longs for is brought to him by the wind (rather like Catherine's in *Wuthering Heights*) or by a ray of light.

Though the poem is slight it is not simple except in theme. The verse form is so constricting that there is, inevitably, some lack of clarity in the actual meaning, and Vaughan's inconsistent use of the pronouns 'you', 'thou' and 'he' does not help. But there is more to the complication than technical problems incompletely solved; there is true ambiguity, as in the highly suggestive line:

> Dayes are my feares.

(c)   *Quickness*

> False life! a foil and no more, when
> Wilt thou be gone?
> Thou foul deception of all men
> That would not have the true come on.

Thou art a Moon-like toil; a blinde
  Self-posing state;
A dark contest of waves and winde;
A meer tempestuous debate.

Life is a fix'd discerning light,
  A knowing Joy;
No chance, or fit: but ever bright,
And calm and full, yet doth not cloy.

Tis such a blissful thing, that still
  Doth vivifie,
And shine and smile, and hath the skil
To please without Eternity.

Thou art a toylsom Mole, or less
  A moving mist
But life is, what none can express,
A quickness, which my God hath kist.

The idea of quickness (life, vitality) was a favourite
concept of Vaughan's, as it naturally would be of a
poet so lovingly preoccupied with nature. Greenness,
growing plants, Spring, early morning, freshness after
rain: all these things inspired both his life and his
poetry.

In attempting to define life Vaughan sets himself as
hard a task as Herbert's when he is trying to describe
prayer. A comparison of the way in which the two poets
handle the problem illuminates the difference between
them. Herbert's *Prayer* is a series of metaphors, twenty-
two in all, if one excludes the line 'Softnesse and
peace . . .' Each is completely precise; any obscurity is
due to the difficulty of the subject, not to any lack of

hard accuracy. *Quickness* works by a totally different method and is an excellent illustration of what Professor Empson said about another poem of Vaughan's: 'It is these evanescent but powerful suggestions that Vaughan gains by blurring the outline and losing the energy of the conceit of Herbert.' It also illustrates Dr Johnson's comment on Vaughan, quoted by Empson: 'He trembles upon the brink of meaning.'

The structure of *Quickness* is firm enough: two verses to describe false life and three to describe true life. But the imagery is certainly blurred. Vaughan's technique is to explain something we know little about in terms of something we know even less about – rather as Keats, in trying to make us hear an unfamiliar sound, the music at a feast in a medieval castle, tells us it is 'yearning like a God in pain', which helps us very much as suggestion and not in the least as information. Much of *Quickness* moves in a world of half-metaphor:

> Life is a fix'd, discerning light,
>   A knowing Joy;

where abstract language and vague concepts are piled up with evocative rather than descriptive force. The third and fourth verses are composed entirely in this way. The reader is being persuaded by a series of emotional words: light, joy, bright, calm, full, blissful, shine, smile.

There is some precise metaphor. 'Foil' in verse 1 most likely means 'anything that sets off something by contrast' though it could possibly mean 'false scent'; the second meaning certainly leads better into the next two lines:

> Thou foul deception of all men
> That would not have the true come on.

'Moon-like toil' is basically a very exact image though the wording is rather misty; a witless expenditure of energy, characteristic of the false life Vaughan is thinking of, is well symbolised by the moon's exertions in pulling the tides backwards and forwards. In the last verse false life is called 'a toylsom Mole' and 'a moving mist'. There is an eloquent gradation here: the mole, however humble he may be, is animate; the mist is less than animate though it moves. Both metaphors are accurate, not least because they have something charming about them, as false life must have if it is to be regarded as a menace at all. Vaughan the country-man must have seen the attraction of moles; we know he liked mists.

All these comparisons lead up to the startling and famous last line of the poem:

> *A quickness, which my God hath kist.*

As a definition of life this tells us nothing and brilliantly suggests everything. It is typical of Vaughan.

SUGGESTED READING

F. C. Hutchinson
   Henry Vaughan: a Life and Interpretation, Oxford, 1947
E. C. Pettet
   Of Paradise and Light, Cambridge, 1960

CHAPTER VI

Andrew Marvell

Andrew Marvell was born in 1621 at Winestead-in-Holderness near Hull, fourth child of the rector of the parish. He was educated at Hull Grammar School and for the rest of his life maintained close links with the city: his father had moved there in 1624, two of his sisters married prominent local citizens and he himself became its Member of Parliament.

He was a clever and studious boy and did well both at school and at Trinity College, Cambridge, where he spent seven years from 1633. He left the university with the reputation of a scholar and added to his accomplishments during the next four years by travelling abroad extensively and becoming an able linguist. By being out of the country at this time he missed most of the Civil War.

In 1650 he was appointed tutor to the twelve-year-old daughter of Lord Fairfax, the Parliamentarian general, who after years of fighting had now settled peacefully in Nunappleton House, on his estate in Yorkshire. He had disapproved of the execution of the King and had subsequently disagreed with Cromwell on other political and military matters, to such an extent that he had resigned. During the following two years, for the first and only time in his adult life,

Marvell lived in the country. The gracious house, its beautiful gardens, meadows and woods, as well as its inhabitants, won his complete affection. Difficult as it is to date Marvell's poems, it is safe to suggest that it was in these years he wrote *Upon Appleton House* and *The Garden*, and probably most of his other well-known lyrics too.

In 1652 his appointment came to an end and he left this country retreat behind to plunge into a world of affairs, in-groups, animosities and hard work. By disposition he was so fair-minded a man with so little of the partisan about him that it is not always easy to say where his political sympathies lay. One of his most remarkable characteristics was that, without being in the least a trimmer, he could so see both sides of any situation that he could adapt himself to most that came his way. Before 1650 he appears to have found the Royalist cause congenial, yet all the time he felt a growing admiration for Cromwell and could also be happy in the household of an eminent Parliamentarian who was Cromwell's enemy. The sanity and balance of his views are fully seen in *An Horatian Ode*.

He now decided to serve the state and asked Milton for help in finding a suitable post. Milton, who was at the time Latin Secretary to the Council of State, wrote an enthusiastic letter to the President of the Council about him, suggesting that he should be made assistant to himself in the Secretaryship. The application was not immediately successful, but in 1657, after Marvell had spent his time very happily as tutor to a ward of Cromwell's, the appointment was made. Marvell's opinion of Milton was even higher than Milton's of

him and the two men worked harmoniously together
until the death of the Protector, in 1658, and the subse-
quent collapse of the Commonwealth changed the
lives of both.

From the time of his leaving Fairfax's employment
and entering a wider world Marvell had been engaged
in writing verse which in no way resembled his great
lyrical poetry. Minor though it was in point of quality
it took up a major part of his energy for the rest of his
career. This verse was occasional and satirical, often
violently so, for Marvell's balance on broader issues
did not mean that he could not express himself with
the greatest energy when some particular point roused
him. He was independent and detached but he was by
no means placid. During the time of the Commonwealth subjects that goaded him into speech were, for
example, the supremacy of the Dutch at sea and
Admiral Blake's fight with the Spanish fleet. After the
Restoration, though he upheld monarchy as an institu-
tion, his favourite subject was the deficiencies of the
Court party. It need hardly be said that these satires
were published anonymously, or circulated only in
manuscript.

Marvell was elected Member of Parliament for Hull
in 1659 and continued to represent the city till his
death in 1678. He sat in three parliaments: Richard
Cromwell's first and last parliament which was dis-
solved in the spring of 1660, the Convention parliament
which existed for the rest of the year and whose chief
function was to negotiate the return of Charles II, and
the first parliament of Charles himself which lasted for
eighteen years, that is, till just after Marvell's death.

Marvell was an ideal M.P., working hard, keeping his constituents fully informed about what went on and showing a steady interest in their concerns. He delivered few speeches in the House but he made his presence felt: we hear of a slanging-match with the Speaker for which he was called to order. He seems to have won general respect: it was surely an honour that he was selected for the 1663 mission to Moscow. But though he and his career survived the Restoration and indeed prospered under it, he did not forget those in danger. In 1660 he exerted himself courageously, and successfully, to save Milton.

During his years in Parliament Marvell became known as a prose pamphleteer. His most famous work in this line is *The Rehearsal Transpros'd*, published in two parts, in 1672 and 1673. It is a spirited plea for religious toleration. Marvell's prose style has been aptly described by Augustine Birrell as 'that of honest men who have something to say'. (Birrell's biography of Marvell, incidentally, though published as early as 1905, is still the best documented and the most interesting. His description of the visit to Moscow is very funny.)

It is almost certain that Marvell never married. After his death a woman who called herself Mary Marvell claimed to be the poet's widow and therefore to be legally in possession of his manuscripts. The matter has been as fully investigated as is now possible and it seems that she may have been a servant of Marvell's trying to make money out of the papers or, as one critic ingeniously suggests, it may have been a publicity stunt on the part of Marvell's publisher. The first edition of the poems appeared in 1681.

The great set-pieces of Marvell's poetry, *To His Coy Mistress*, *The Garden* and *An Horatian Ode*, have come in for an excessive amount of attention and analysis, and often far-fetched interpretation. *Upon Appleton House*, one of the finest things he wrote, is so long and varied that extracts from it give only a limited impression. So let us examine two poems which though well-known have not been quite so exposed to comment as the first three: *The Definition of Love* and *Bermudas*.

(a)   *The Definition of Love*

My Love is of a birth as rare
As 'tis for object strange and high:
It was begotten by despair
Upon Impossibility.

Magnanimous Despair alone
Could show me so divine a thing,
Where feeble Hope could ne'r have flown
But vainly flapt its Tinsel Wing.

And yet I quickly might arrive
Where my extended Soul is fixt,
But Fate does Iron wedges drive,
And alwaies crouds it self betwixt.

For Fate with jealous Eye does see
Two perfect Loves; nor lets them close:
Their union would her ruine be,
And her Tyrannick pow'r depose.

And therefore her Decrees of Steel
Us as the distant Poles have plac'd,
(Though Loves whole World on us doth wheel)
Not by themselves to be embrac'd.

Unless the giddy Heav'n fall,
And Earth some new Convulsion tear;
And, us to joyn, the World should all
Be cramp'd into a *Planisphere*.

As Lines so Loves *oblique* may well
Themselves in every Angle greet:
But ours so truly *Paralel*,
Though infinite can never meet.

Therefore the Love which us doth bind,
But Fate so enviously debarrs,
Is the Conjunction of the Mind,
And Opposition of the Stars.

As Herbert tries to define prayer, and Vaughan life,
Marvell here attempts to define love. Though he speaks
from and about his own experience, it is not just a
personal love poem; he has something more general
and indeed universal in mind. His definition springs
from the combination of hard thinking and tender
feeling which is characteristic of Metaphysical poetry.

The poem read today suffers from the changes that
have taken place in the language since the seventeenth
century. Words like 'extended', 'union' and 'enviously'
have lost much of their richness and suggestion. This
of course applies to nearly all poetry of the period but
this poem suffers more than most because it also con-
tains technical vocabulary the meaning of which needs
a note and which, because it is not part of the reader's
natural vocabulary, can never make a spontaneous
impact on him. An example is the key word 'planisphere'. Most of us have seen astrolabes in museums

and would get some immediate impression from a
mention of them, but 'planisphere' does not give us the
jolt that Marvell intended. 'Conjunction' and 'opposition' mean something to everyone and that something
is certainly part of the point, but only a small part
compared with the wealth of significance in the terms
as used astronomically. We see how much we are
hampered when we look for contrast at the geometri-
cal image, where the central words 'oblique' and
'parallel' are part of our everyday thinking and where
therefore we immediately share Marvell's idea.

In spite of this handicap the poem, though presenting difficulties quite apart from its vocabulary, is strong
and impressive. As in so many metaphysical poems the
structure is that of an argument; not an argument
with two premises and a conclusion like that of *To his
Coy Mistress* but a series of reasoned statements of more
or less equal weight and of cumulative effect, not
exactly leading up to but culminating in a decisive last
verse. This verse starts with a logical 'therefore', though
in fact what it says is a repetition rather than a conclusion: its paraphrasable 'meaning' is just the same as
that of, for example, verse 4:

> For Fate with jealous Eye does see
> Two perfect Loves; nor lets them close:
> Their union would her ruine be,
> And her Tyrannick pow'r depose ...
>
> Therefore the Love which us doth bind,
> But Fate so enviously debarrs,
> Is the Conjunction of the Mind,
> And Opposition of the Stars.

Psychologically the poem is very sound, based as it is on a highly realistic ambiguity. Marvell's intention surely is to goad us into opposition and into disagreeing with his apparent conclusion that true love is negative rather than positive – or rather positive in a way that involves negation; yet his ostensible viewpoint does meet with a certain straightforward response. However much mortal lovers thrive on fulfilment and actuality, everyone knows the perverse pleasure of renunciation and has experienced at some time the neurotic wish to stave off success.

It is from this entirely natural ambivalence that the paradoxes of the poem spring and they therefore carry genuine emotion with them and are not mere intellectual quibbling. And this is just as well, otherwise a very arid set of verses would be the result, for the poem in itself is one long paradox and is made up of short paradoxes: 'Magnanimous Despair', a paradox to begin with, begets a child on Impossibility, a conception which would not have a very long life and yet the poet's love is seen to survive everything; the one condition which could unite the North and South Pole would be a total collapse of the globe which would automatically annihilate them; and so on.

If paradox is the most important technical device of *The Definition*, personification comes next. Fate is a particularly interesting character; he is a complete being, human or super-human, with a jealous eye and an unpleasant dog-in-the-manger attitude, who drives wedges into things, like a navvy or like Vulcan and shoves loving couples apart. Dr Christopher Hill in his essay on 'Society and Andrew Marvell' (in the Penguin

Critical Anthology) has some illuminating things to say about Marvell's Fate. He sees it as the 'historic process' which can militate against Love, literally militate as he associates Marvell's Fate, convincingly, with the 'blind forces of the Civil War', and several times he insists on Marvell's awareness of the realities of his day and of how love is indeed at the mercy of the outer world.

Other characters, as well as Despair and Impossibility, are the conventional Hope with conventional but charming 'Tinsel Wing', Heaven, Earth and of course Love itself. In assigning to Love the normal conception of a mammal, Marvell is following the well-established tradition which gives parents to abstract qualities, for example, Milton's

> Hence, loathèd Melancholy
> Of Cerberus and blackest Midnight born

and Samuel Daniel's

> Care-charmer Sleep, son of the sable Night,
> Brother to Death.

But by wording it more plainly, more crudely even:

> It was begotten by Despair
> Upon Impossibility,

he makes the reader think of real, not fanciful, begetting and so adds human emotion to a subject which certainly calls for it but could so easily be robbed of it by intellectualism.

The tone of the *Definition* is above all reasonable and mature. The fact that it should be so is a mark of the poem's success, for the content, when paraphrased, is an expression of exaggerated and intemperate passion. The skill of the technique and the sheer sophistication of the approach – comparable to those of *An Horatian Ode* where the material dealt with is even more inflammable – give the poem its strength and control, and, paradoxically, its passion.

(*b*)   *Bermudas*

Where the remote *Bermudas* ride
In th' Oceans bosome unespy'd,
From a small Boat, that row'd along,
The listning Winds receiv'd this song.
    What should we do but sing his Praise
That led us through the watry Maze,
Unto an Isle so long unknown,
And yet far kinder than our own?
Where he the huge Sea-Monsters wracks,
That lift the Deep upon their Backs.
He lands us on a grassy Stage;
Safe from the Storms, and Prelat's rage.
He gave us this eternal Spring,
Which here enamells every thing;
And sends the Fowl's to us in care,
On daily Visits through the Air.
He hangs in shades the Orange bright,
Like golden Lamps in a green night.
And does in the Pomegranates close,
Jewels more rich than *Ormus* show's.
He makes the Figs our mouths to meet;
And throws the Melons at our feet.
But Apples plants of such a price,
No Tree could ever bear them twice.

With Cedars, chosen by his hand
From *Lebanon*, he stores the Land.
And makes the hollow Seas, that roar,
Proclaim the Ambergris on shoar.
He cast (of which we rather boast)
The Gospels Pearl upon our Coast.
And in these Rocks for us did frame
A Temple, where to sound his Name.
Oh let our Voice his Praise exalt
Till it arrive at Heavens Vault:
Which thence (perhaps) rebounding, may
Eccho beyond the *Mexique Bay*.
Thus sung they, in the *English* boat,
An holy and a chearful Note,
And all the way, to guide their Chime,
With falling Oars they kept the time.

This poem is based on historical events which took place in Marvell's time. The Bermudas, which had been discovered at the beginning of the sixteenth century, had become in the seventeenth century a haven for those who were escaping from the persecutions of Laud. Marvell knew people who had actually been there and his interest must have been further stimulated by Cromwell's sending ships there in 1651 to gain support for the Puritan cause. So his involvement was not academic but warm and personal. The subject, however, was by no means as fraught as that of his other historical poem *An Horatian Ode*. In *Bermudas* he has scope for indignation about the 'Prelat's Rage' (bishops infuriated him) which had made exile necessary for some; but his anger is straightforward and the harmony of the poem as a whole springs not only from the peace of mind of the exiles but from his own lack of conflict on the subject.

To suggest that the poem is a working song, as Christopher Hill does, is going too far; it is no sea-shanty. Nevertheless the singers are the reverse of lotus-eaters; they are rowing vigorously and purposefully; they have recently of their own volition undergone the dangers of crossing the Atlantic; and they are unselfishly grateful for their present happiness. The tone of their song is Puritanical, not only 'chearful' but 'holy'. God is reverently praised for all the details of their lot. He is credited with having done everything personally and his tasks are made to sound energetic and exhausting. Yet, and this is not typically Puritanical, what they first and chiefly thank him for is the beauty of their surroundings, the weather, the fruit, the trees. The descriptions are loving and sensuous:

> He hangs in shades the Orange bright,
> Like golden Lamps in a green Night;

they recall *The Garden* and the lusher passages of *Upon Appleton House*. The exiles' allusion to the presence of Christianity on the island is cursory and cool by comparison:

> He cast (of which we rather boast)
> The Gospels Pearl upon our Coast.
> And in these rocks for us did frame
> A Temple, where to sound his Name.

Marvell's picture of this earthly paradise is not complicated by the suggestions of menace that we find in

The Garden and *Upon Appleton House*. In *Bermudas* he describes the fruit as coming to the eaters rather than the
usual way round:

> He makes the Figs our mouths to meet;
> And throws the Melons at our feet.

He presents this fancy in *The Garden*, too, but danger
enters into the situation: the melons do not merely lie
at your feet ready to be eaten; they trip you up:

> The Luscious Clusters of the Vine
> Upon my Mouth do crush their Wine;
> The Nectaren, and curious Peach,
> Into my hands themselves do reach;
> Stumbling on Melons, as I pass,
> Insnar'd with Flow'rs, I fall on Grass.

The danger in *Bermudas* has been surmounted, seem-
ingly for ever.

> ... he the huge Sea-Monsters wracks,
> That lift the Deep upon their backs.
> He lands us on a grassy Stage;
> Safe from the Storms.

In *Bermudas* Marvell uses the four-foot iambic couplet
which we meet in many of his other poems. He states
that the song is one to which the rowers can time their
strokes and if we were to take this literally we should
expect less variety than we find in, for example, *To his
Coy Mistress*. But the idea is merely a convention; the
prologue and epilogue do not differ rhythmically
from the song itself and there is no attempt at the sort
of dramatisation which would call for effects of

rhythm. The verse *is* in fact less subtle than that of *To his Coy Mistress* but this is because the subject matter is less subtle, not for any onomatopoeic reasons. The rhythm of the song itself is far from regular, which improves the poem but which would have been fatal to row to.

Bermudas is not one of Marvell's greatest poems, for its scope is limited, but it displays most of the characteristics which make the others so great.

SUGGESTED READING

ed. W. H. Bagguley
   Andrew Marvell. Tercentenary Tributes, O.U.P., 1922
Augustine Birrell
   Andrew Marvell, Macmillan, 1950
ed. John Carey
   Andrew Marvell (Penguin Critical Anthologies), Penguin, 1969
Pierre Legouis
   Andrew Marvell: Poet, Puritan, Patriot, O.U.P., 1965
ed. Michael Wilding
   Marvell (Modern Judgements), Macmillan, 1969

CHAPTER VII

The Metaphysical Poets and the Twentieth Century

The twentieth-century discovery of the Metaphysical Poets was to an extent anticipated in the nineteenth century by the emerging reputation of Marvell as a poet. In his own day he had no such reputation, that is, as far as his best, his lyrical poetry, was concerned; it was only as a satirist that he was known. His was quite a different case from that of Donne, whose poetry was very popular during his lifetime and immediately after but made hardly any general impression on the next two centuries though some distinguished individuals thought highly of it. But from the early eighteen-hundreds Marvell's fame steadily rose. Lamb spoke of him with real warmth. Hazlitt praised his work though seeming not to know much about it. Gerard Manley Hopkins frequently quoted him. Tennyson was given to reciting *To his Coy Mistress*. All this makes him sound like a poet's poet and indeed in the nineteenth century this is what he appears to have been. There were many dissenting voices among men of letters who were not poets, for example, Gosse, and the anthologists were extremely wary about including him and in particular fought shy of *To his Coy Mistress*.

Significantly, the prophet had honour outside his own country. Throughout this period American critics were much more enthusiastic and knowledgeable about Marvell than the British. Edgar Allan Poe, especially, wrote most perceptively about him.

In England, what made Marvell the first Metaphysical to be appreciated and what made the appreciation so limited was perhaps the same factor. The name of Andrew Marvell had been kept alive during the centuries when Donne, Vaughan and Herbert were far from being household words. Marvell's name *was* a household word, but not as the name of a poet. From the time of his death, and indeed before, he had been quoted as a symbol of integrity and patriotism, by Wordsworth, for example; he was the archetypal great mind, the fighter for freedom, the brave and just man. The others had no such claims made for them. They were to depend for their rehabilitation on the Grierson anthology and the Eliot essay, and so did Marvell too for a full recognition of his *poetic* stature.

Today Donne and Marvell are by far the most popular of the Metaphysical Poets. Books and essays appear about them every year. Little, comparatively, is written about Vaughan, Herbert, Carew, Crashaw and the others. In the case of these others, this is because they are not major poets and have surged forward from obscurity with their betters. Herbert and Vaughan, who could well be called major poets, have never appealed to twentieth-century taste as much as Marvell and Donne have, though discerning critics have rated them very highly indeed. Their tone and their subject matter limit their audience; they hardly ever raise their voices and they say a great deal about religion and almost nothing overtly about sex.

F. O. Matthiessen, in the first chapter of *The Achievement of T. S. Eliot*, attributes the rise of the Metaphysicals, and particularly that of Donne, almost exclusively to the influence not only of Eliot's preaching but his practice:

> Donne has assumed the stature of a centrally important figure for the first time since the seventeenth century; and his rise has been directly connected with the fact that Eliot has enabled us to see him with fresh closeness, not only by means of his analysis of the method of metaphysical poetry but also because he has renewed that method in the rhythms and imagery of his own verse.

Matthiessen speaks interestingly too of the earlier popularity of the Metaphysicals in America:

> It is increasingly apparent that the renaissance of the New England mind, from Emerson and Thoreau to Emily Dickinson, felt a deep kinship with the long buried modes of thought and feeling of the seventeenth century; in fact, Emily Dickinson's poetry, especially, must be described as metaphysical.

He points out that Eliot's influence in England could have done little unless there had been a widespread predisposition, similar to that in America, towards these poets:

> The jagged brokenness of Donne's thought has struck a responsive note in our age, for we have seen a reflection of our own problem in the manner in

which his passionate mind, unable to find any final truth in which it could rest, became fascinated with the process of thought itself.

But Matthiessen includes a warning note. He is still speaking specifically of Donne but the comment applies equally to all the Metaphysical Poets:

It may be that in reaction against Donne's previous neglect our generation has gone to the extreme of exaggerating his importance.

And this note is heard also in an essay by Eliot himself 'Donne in our Time':

Donne's poetry is a concern of the present and the recent past, rather than of the future;

and later:

We may even say with some confidence that we probably understand sympathetically Donne to-day better than poets and critics fifty years hence will understand him.

Eliot is careful to explain, however, that it is not just a question of fashion:

I by no means wish to affirm that the importance of a particular poet, or of a particular type of poetry, is merely a matter of capricious fashion. I wish simply to distinguish between the absolute and the relative in popularity, and to recognise in the relative (both when a poet is unduly preferred and when he is unduly ignored) an element of the reasonable, the just and the significant.

Eliot's view is, I am sure, correct as far as concerns the Metaphysical Poets. There are many things in our world which make us turn to them with recognition and appreciation and these things may pass away. But Eliot is convinced, and again I am sure he is right, that never again will these poets sink into oblivion or even be underestimated. Their place is assured now.

To define the characteristics which modern poetry and metaphysical poetry have in common would be to repeat most of the points made in earlier chapters. It is more useful to demonstrate by the examination of specific poems what happened to poetry in the course of the last three centuries which made the Metaphysicals undervalued for so long and then so warmly praised.

Two of the most famous and powerful poems of the early seventeenth century were about the death of a loved one: Donne's *A Nocturnall upon S. Lucies day* and Henry King's *The Exequy*. If from a reading of these poems we pass to Dryden's *To the Memory of Mr. Oldham*, written not much later, there is no need for comment on the dramatic change that had already taken place. It declares itself.

> Farewell, too little and too lately known,
> Whom I began to think and call my own:
> For sure our souls were near alli'd, and thine
> Cast in the same poetic mould with mine.
> One common note on either lyre did strike,
> And knaves and fools we both abhorr'd alike.
> To the same goal did both our studies drive;
> The last set out the soonest did arrive.

Thus Nisus fell upon the slippery place,
Whilst his young friend perform'd and won the race.
O early ripe! to thy abundant store
What could advancing age have added more?
It might (what Nature never gives the young)
Have taught the numbers of thy native tongue.
But satire needs not these, and wit will shine
Through the harsh cadence of a rugged line.
A noble error, and but seldom made,
When poets are by too much force betrayed.
Thy gen'rous fruits, though gather'd ere their
    prime,
Still showed a quickness; and maturing Time
But mellows what we write to the dull sweets of
    rhyme.
Once more, hail and farewell! farewell, thou
    young,
But ah! too short, Marcellus of our tongue!
Thy brows with ivy and with laurel bound;
But Fate and gloomy Night encompass thee around.

If then we read Pope's *Elegy to the Memory of an Unfortunate Lady*, Shelley's *Adonais* and some of Tennyson's *In Memoriam*, which has already provided such excellent grounds of comparison, we see poetry getting farther and farther away from what it had been when Donne and Henry King were speaking to their contemporaries. The nineteenth century was the farthest point of all and just after the end of it there came, with the work of Eliot and Pound, the poetic revolution which brought readers close to the Metaphysicals again.

Here a comparison of nineteenth-century poems

with twentieth-century ones where the subject matter is similar demonstrates the point. Shelley's *Ozymandias* and Ted Hughes's *Relic* present much the same theme: the inexorable rhythm of power where what destroyed and was feared yesterday is itself destroyed today, and so on to the end of time. Their methods are entirely different.

(a)   *Ozymandias*

I met a traveller from an antique land
Who said: Two vast and trunkless legs of stone
Stand in the desert. Near them, on the sand,
Half sunk, a shattered visage lies, whose frown,
And wrinkled lip, and sneer of cold command,
Tell that its sculptor well those passions read
Which yet survive, stamped on these lifeless things,
The hand that mocked them, and the heart that
      fed:
And on the pedestal these words appear:
'My name is Ozymandias, king of kings:
Look on my works, ye Mighty, and despair!'
Nothing beside remains. Round the decay
Of that colossal wreck, boundless and bare,
The lone and level sands stretch far away.

(b)   *Relic*

I found this jawbone at the sea's edge:
There, crabs, dogfish, broken by the breakers or
      tossed
To flap for half an hour and turn to a crust
Continue the beginning. The deeps are cold:

In that darkness camaraderie does not hold:
Nothing touches but, clutching, devours. And the
    jaws,
Before they are satisfied or their stretched purpose
Slacken, go down jaws; go gnawn bare. Jaws
Eat and are finished and the jawbone comes to the
    beach:
This is the sea's achievement; with shells,
Vertebrae, claws, carapaces, skulls.

Time in the sea eats its tail, thrives, casts these
Indigestibles, the spars of purposes
That failed far from the surface. None grow rich
In the sea. This curved jawbone did not laugh
But gripped, gripped and is now a cenotaph.

Wordsworth in *London 1802* and Thom Gunn in *My Sad Captains* both feel the need of a leader to turn to in difficult times. Wordsworth's choice is Milton; Thom Gunn has several, unnamed and less heroic, but performing the same function and thought of in the same metaphor, as stars.

(*a*)   *London 1802*

Milton! thou shouldst be living at this hour:
England hath need of thee: she is a fen
Of stagnant waters: altar, sword, and pen,
Fireside, the heroic wealth of hall and bower,
Have forfeited their ancient English dower
Of inward happiness. We are selfish men;
Oh! raise us up, return to us again;
And give us manners, virtue, freedom, power.

Thy soul was like a Star, and dwelt apart;
Thou hadst a voice whose sound was like the sea:
Pure as the naked heavens, majestic, free,
So didst thou travel on life's common way,
In cheerful godliness; and yet thy heart
The lowliest duties on herself did lay.

(b)   *My Sad Captains*

One by one they appear in
the darkness: a few friends, and
a few with historical
names. How late they start to shine!
but before they fade they stand
perfectly embodied, all

the past lapping them like a
cloak of chaos. They were men
who, I thought, lived only to
renew the wasteful force they
spent with each hot convulsion.
They remind me, distant now.

True, they are not at rest yet,
but now that they are indeed
apart, winnowed from failures,
they withdraw to an orbit
and turn with disinterested
hard energy, like the stars.

A particularly illuminating comparison, it seems to
me, is provided by two poems about gipsies, one by
Wordsworth, the other by Ezra Pound.

(a)   *Gipsies*

Yet are they here the same unbroken knot
Of human beings, in the self-same spot!
   Men, women, children, yea, the frame
   Of the whole spectacle the same!
Only their fire seems bolder, yielding light,
Now deep and red, the colouring of night,
   That on their gipsy-faces falls,
   Their bed of straw and blanket-walls,
Twelve hours, twelve bounteous hours are gone, while I
     while I
Have been a traveller under open sky,
   Much witnessing of change and cheer,
   Yet as I left I find them here!
The weary sun betook himself to rest,
Then issued vesper from the fulgent west,
   Outshining like a visible god
   The glorious path in which he trod.
And now, ascending, after one dark hour
And one night's diminution of her power,
   Behold the mighty moon! this way
   She looks as if at them – but they
Regard not her: oh better wrong and strife,
(By nature transient) than such torpid life;
   Life which the very stars reprove
   As on their silent tasks they move!
Yet witness all that stirs in heaven or earth!
In scorn I speak not; they are what their birth
     birth
   And breeding suffer them to be;
   Wild outcasts of society!

(b)   *The Gypsy*

That was the top of the walk, when he said:
'Have you seen any others, any of our lot,
With apes or bears?'
    – a brown upstanding fellow
Not like the half-castes,
    up on the wet road near Clermont.
The wind came, and the rain,
And mist clotted about the trees in the valley,
And I'd the long ways behind me,
    gray Arles and Biaucaire,
And he said, 'Have you seen any of our lot?'
I'd seen a lot of his lot . . .
    ever since Rhodez,
Coming down from the fair
    of St. John,
With caravans, but never an ape or a bear.

There is no question, in any of these cases, of comparing (a) with (b) in order to make value judgements.
For one thing it would be difficult to say which of the
pair was the better poem, as they are all good examples
of their genre, and in any case that would not be the
point. In reading them it is immediately possible to feel
the change that twentieth-century poets have brought
about and the way in which they cope with experiences
that earlier poets encountered but with which they
dealt quite differently. And all these differences link
the poets of our own day with the Metaphysical Poets.
    To begin with, if it is true, as was discussed in Chapter
I, that there ought to be 'a note of tension or strain' in
any poetry that can accurately be called metaphysical,

then the (b) poems are more metaphysical than the (a) poems. Shelley sounds world-weary and Wordsworth, in *London 1802*, disgruntled and, in *Gipsies*, complacent; they do not write like men under stress. Ted Hughes and Thom Gunn do, while Ezra Pound seems to be grappling with some vast ambiguity.

Shelley and Wordsworth speak magisterially, that is, on the strength of their previous thinking and meditation; they have come to conclusions. The authors of the (b) poems appear to be thinking as they write, which does not make them less eloquent or more eloquent, but more immediate. Interestingly, Shelley's and Wordsworth's opening lines are worded with something like the early seventeenth-century immediacy: 'I met a traveller . . .', 'Yet are they here . . .' but the effect is soon belied. Shelley presents his thoughts at two removes, by way of the traveller and the inscription. Wordsworth distances his reflections by means of various rhetorical devices. The immediacy of the (b) poems persists throughout. Syntactically Ted Hughes's first line, 'I found this jawbone . . .' is exactly like Shelley's, but in the last line the poet is still holding and looking at the bone.

It follows that to twentieth-century readers the (b) poems are psychologically more interesting; we have come to demand and to enjoy the experience of hearing a poet exploring his own mind and heart, seeming to work out the sum as he goes along, not just giving us the answer. The techniques of both groups of poems are naturally part of their respective approaches to the subject matter. The (a) poems with their faultless iambics and their traditional verse forms, regularly followed, have a set, final sound which goes with their meaning. The (b) poems are much more fluid. There is pattern, of course, and discipline; Thom Gunn's syllabics, the free verse of Ezra Pound and Ted Hughes, though highly individual because formulated by themselves to suit their own poetic needs of the moment, are carried out with scrupulous craftsmanship. But it is the rhythm of the thought and feeling, as with the Metaphysicals, that is the guiding principle.

Experienced readers no doubt get pleasure from both the (a) and the (b) poems, but many who might have to make conscious adjustments to appreciate Wordsworth's *Gipsies* would find spontaneous excitement in Pound's *The Gypsy*. It is this kind of spontaneity which marks the modern response to the Metaphysical Poets. We are lucky in being able for the present to react instinctively to them and should make the most of the experience. It may not last long, though their achievement will.

SUGGESTED READING

Cleanth Brooks
  Modern Poetry and the Tradition, Poetry London, 1948
Donald Davie
  Articulate Energy, Routledge, 1955
T. S. Eliot
  'Donne in our Time' from *A Garland for John Donne*,
  ed. Theodore Spencer, Gloucester, Mass., 1958
F. R. Leavis
  New Bearings in English Poetry, Chatto, 1932

F. O. Matthiessen
   The Achievement of T. S. Eliot, O.U.P., 1958
George Williamson
   'Donne and the Poetry of Today', from *A Garland for John Donne* (see above)

Index

Eliot, T. S.: *The Metaphysical Poets*, 3
12; *Prufrock*, 6; 21, 25, 26; *For
Lancelot Andrewes*, 28; *After Strange
Gods*, 32; *Andrew Marvell*, 33;
Whispers of Immortality, 42; 68, 100;
Donne in our Time, 102; 103, 104
Emerson, Ralph Waldo, 101
Empson, William, 25; *Seven Types of
Ambiguity*, 59; 69, 82
Enright, D. J., 59
Essex, Earl of, 37

Fairfax, Lord, 85, 86, 87
Felltham, Owen: *When, Dearest, I but
think on thee*, 21
Ferrar, Nicholas, 57

Gardner, Professor Helen: *The Meta-
physical Poets*, 2; 23
Godolphin, Sidney, 1
Goethe, 4
Gosse, Edmund, 99
Grierson, Sir Herbert: *Metaphysical
Lyrics and Poems of the Seventeenth
Century*, 2; 3, 100
Gunn, Thom, 106; *My Sad Captains*,
107; 110, 111

Habington, William, 1
Hall, John, 1; *The Call*, 19; *On an
Hourglasse*, 22
Hazlitt, William, 99
Herbert, George, 1: *The Flower*, 14;
The Pulley, 26, 63, 64; *Aaron*, 26; 29,
32, 55–70; *The Temple*, 57, 59; *A
Priest to the Temple*, 57; *Redemption*,
59–63; *The Agonie*, 60; *The Sacrifice*,
60; *Love*, 62; *The Collar*, 62, 64;
Jordan (I), 63–7; *The Pearl*, 65;
Affliction, 65; *Dulnesse*, 66; *Jordan (II)*,
66; *Death*, 67–70; 73, 75, 76; *Prayer*,
81; 90, 100, 101
Herbert, Jane, *née* Danvers, 56, 57
Herbert, Magdalen, later Danvers,
55, 56
Heyrick, Thomas, 29
Heywood, Elizabeth, 35
Heywood, Jasper, 36
Heywood, John, 35

Hill, Christopher: *Society and Andrew
Marvell*, 92; 96
Hobbes, Thomas, 4
Hopkins, Gerard Manley: *Hurrahing
in Harvest*, 47; *Felix Randal*, 47; 48,
58, 99
Howard of Effingham, Lord, 37
Hughes, Ted: *Relic*, 105–6; 110,
111
Hull, 85, 87
Hutchinson, F. E., 73

James I, 39, 40
Johnson, Dr Samuel: *Life of Cowley*,
2; 3, 5, 23, 82

Keats, John: *The Eve of St. Agnes*, 82
King, Henry, 1, 22; *The Exequy*, 26–8;
29, 103, 104

Lamb, Charles, 99
Laud, Archbishop, 95
Leighton, 56
Lincoln's Inn, 36, 37
Llansantffraed, 74
London, 36, 71
Lucretius, 4, 6

Marvell, Andrew, 1, 11: *The Nymph
complaining for the death of her Faun*, 15;
*A Dialogue between the Resolved Soul
and Created Pleasure*, 17–18; *Upon
Appleton House*, 24, 26, 86, 96, 97;
An Horatian Ode, 26, 86, 89, 94, 95;
29, 32, 69, 85–98; *The Garden*, 86, 89,
96, 97; *The Rehearsal Transpros'd*, 88;
To his Coy Mistress, 89, 91, 97, 98;
The Definition of Love, 89–94; *Ber-
mudas*, 94–8; 99, 100
'Marvell, Mary', 88
Matthiessen, F. O.: *The Achievement of
T. S. Eliot*, 101–2
Milton, John: *Paradise Lost*, 4; 11;
Comus, 58; *Lycidas*, 65; 86, 87;
L'Allegro, 93
Mitcham, 38, 39, 40
Montgomery Castle, 55
More, Sir Thomas, 35
Moscow, 88

Casebook Series

GENERAL EDITOR: A. E. Dyson

IN PREPARATION

Charlotte Brontë: *'Jane Eyre' and 'Villette'* MIRIAM ALLOTT
Coleridge: *The Ancient Mariner and Other Poems* ALUN R. JONES and
  WILLIAM TYDEMAN
Conrad: *The Secret Agent* IAN WATT
Donne: *Songs and Sonnets* JULIAN LOVELOCK
George Eliot: *Middlemarch* PATRICK SWINDEN
James Joyce: *Portrait of the Artist as a Young Man* MORRIS BEJA
Milton: *Paradise Lost* A. E. DYSON
Milton: *Samson Agonistes* STANLEY FISH
Shakespeare: *Richard II* NICHOLAS BROOKE

Modern Judgements Series

GENERAL EDITOR: P. N. Furbank

Dickens   A. E. Dyson
Henry James   Tony Tanner
Milton   Alan Rudrum
Sean O'Casey   Ronald Ayling
Pasternak   Donald Davie and Angela Livingstone
Walter Scott   D. D. Devlin
Racine   R. C. Knight
Shelley   R. B. Woodings
Swift   A. Norman Jeffares
Ford Madox Ford   Richard A. Cassell
Marvell   M. Wilding

TITLES IN PREPARATION INCLUDE

Freud   F. Cioffi